Mount

W9-ABM-523

MILWAUKEE 10. WISCONSIN

Mount Mary College
LIBRARY
MILWAUKEE 15, WISCONSIN

Josephine Van Dyke Brownson

By WALTER ROMIG

Foreword by Most Rev. John Francis O'Hara, C.S.C.
Archbishop of Philadelphia

19 55

THE GABRIEL RICHARD PRESS · DETROIT

64- 240

COPYRIGHT 1955 BY GABRIEL RICHARD PRESS
1234 Washington Boulevard
Detroit 26, Michigan

Published with Ecclesiastical Approval

PRINTED AND BOUND IN THE U. S. A. BY
KINGSPORT PRESS, INC., KINGSPORT, TENN.

921
3824R

TO
Elizabeth Van Dyke Brownson
WHOSE LOYALTY TO THE MEMORY OF

HER SISTER

INSPIRED THE WRITING

OF

THIS BIOGRAPHY

Foreword

"THEY CAN'T HAVE THEM! THEY ARE OURS!"

This cry of indignation came from the heart of Josephine Brownson when she read an article in a Detroit newspaper describing the social service work done by a Protestant church for the children of Catholic immigrants. And she did something about it—something magnificent—and that is what this splendid book is about.

The power of indignation is all too rare these days, and as a result our country is in danger. The people who built the American Republic have not always left sons and daughters to defend its ideals. Even worse, some of the descendants of our early Americans are among the anti-anti-Communists today who are hindering the effort to rid our government of communist spies and traitors.

Like her grandfather Orestes, Josephine Brownson had the power of indignation and the strong will to carry through a program of action. On her mother's side she had the artistic talent and the imagination of the Desnoyers and the tenacity of the Van Dyke. The Religious of the Sacred Heart, Josephine's teachers, brought these excellent qualities to flower. (Her later training for the profession of teaching she received at the Detroit Normal Training School and the University of Michigan.)

What Josephine did about the immigrant children was begin to teach them catechism. She did it herself and she inspired other public school teachers to teach religion. She trained teachers to be catechists, she wrote textbooks for her work, she persuaded the Detroit Board of Education to permit the use of public school buildings after school hours for the classes, and she financed the work, both by the use of her own salary as a public school teacher and by gifts from friends and benefactors.

For thirty-three years she conducted this work—from 1906 to 1939, when her organization was incorporated into the Confraternity of Christian Doctrine under His Eminence Cardinal Mooney. At the peak of the work it had under instruction more than fourteen thousand children with four hundred and fifty-four teachers operating in seventy-five Catechetical Centers. It was all a labor of love. There was no external compulsion on either teachers or children. And its influence went far beyond the city and the archdiocese of Detroit, for as the work became known, Miss Brownson was called here and there over the country, and even to Venezuela, to explain the work and give impulse to catechetical instruction.

His Holiness Pope Pius XI honored Josephine Brownson with the Cross "Pro Ecclesia et Pontifice" in 1933, and that same year she received an honorary doctorate from the University of Detroit. In 1939 she was awarded the Laetare Medal by the University of Notre Dame; her father, Major Henry Brownson, had received that same honor in 1892; her grandfather, Orestes A. Brownson, is buried in the crypt of Sacred Heart Church at Notre Dame.

But earthly honors meant little to her. Her quest was souls to lead to God. God blessed her zeal and gave her her heart's desire. Her harvest was a thousand-fold.

✠ JOHN FRANCIS O'HARA, C.S.C.

Contents

CHAPTER ONE

"From these Roots"

JOSEPHINE VAN DYKE BROWNSON WAS AWARDED THE cross Pro Ecclesia et Pontifice by His Holiness Pope Pius XI in 1933. Later that year, the University of Detroit conferred an honorary doctorate upon her. And in 1939, she was chosen as the Laetare Medalist by the University of Notre Dame.

Such recognition in the divers fields of religion, of education, and of social service, national and international, predicate a depth of character and a breadth of achievement that are rare.

What was the unique nature, the lasting value of her accomplishments? What forces went into the molding of her character? A character that enabled her to discern her vocation in early youth. To pursue it with such steadfastness, with such wisdom and thoroughness that her works became world honored. A character such that when her hour of crisis came upon her, alone and unafraid, she faced God and man with the valiant decision.

Three racial strains combined in her: English, French, and Dutch. In each strain her forebears achieved distinction in their respective professions of letters, the arts, and law. And while differing in vocation, the three had boldly evident characteristics in common. Each was adventurous in spirit and ardently freedom loving. And each had a will of iron. From the earlier settled and hence more cultured East, each was a pioneer to the Western frontier fort of the Colonies,—Detroit. There, each made a name for himself, while contributing to the culture of the young community. And by the eventual union of their blood, they fashioned the character and thus the destiny of Josephine Brownson.

Taking them in turn, there were first the Brownsons.

"The name of Brownson, Bronson, Brunston or Branston, is believed by most historians to have derived from the English name of Branston, which was taken by its first bearers because of their residence at a place of that name in Staffordshire, England. It is found in ancient English and early American records in various spellings." [1]

The first of the family to come to America was John Brownson. With his brother Richard, he emigrated from County Suffolk, England, to the village of Hartford, in Connecticut, in 1636.

Since the family history records no details of the voyage over, we are given to understand that it was comparatively uneventful. But anyone who has enjoyed the week of luxury crossing the Atlantic in a modern steel hulled, diesel driven, eighty thousand ton ship will appreciate the adventurous spirit of those who placed themselves at the mercy of gale winds and mountainous waves in a sixty-foot wooden sailing vessel for forty-five days. Their crossing alone required courage.

Of course, these Puritans did not come to the New World to seek wealth or ease or pleasure. They came to found a new state to be built upon their strict religious principles.

Their leader on the voyage over, and later their pastor in Hartford, was the Reverend Thomas Hooker. He is still

[1] Julius Gay. *Brownson Manuscript Genealogy*. Connecticut Historical Society, Hartford.

remembered in history for having recommended to his flock a democratic form of government much like that under which we now live.[2]

John Brownson served in the war against the Pequot (whom the genius of James Fenimore Cooper has made better known as the Mohican) Indians, and in 1639 is listed among the returning veterans who "by courtesie of the towne" were privileged to "fetch wood and keep swine and cowes on the common" of the village of Hartford. He moved to Farmington in 1652 and was one of the seven founders of the Puritan church there. Nor was the Reverend Hooker's influence otherwise lost on him, for at the session of 1651, and several subsequent ones until his death in 1680, he served as deputy to the General Court of Connecticut.[3]

From his son John there followed in direct male succession seven generations. But, as brief as history is regarding most of them, we must be briefer. Indeed, so brief as to mention merely their names: Isaac, Samuel, Elijah, Noadiah. And fifth in line, without benefit of the Old Testament, came Sylvester. To his son he gave the name of Daphnis. But a merciful Providence intervened and commuted the sentence to Orestes. Thus history has recorded (and recorded indelibly) the name of Orestes as the father of Henry Brownson. And Henry in turn became the father of Josephine. Orestes died in the home of Henry, and within four years of Josephine's birth.

Thus, from her earliest childhood she basked in the reflected brilliance of a paternal grandfather whose "multifarious writings on history, sociology, religion, on politics, art, and philosophy had given him a world-name." [4]

[2] R. P. Halleck. *History of American Literature.* p. 16, New York. 1912.
[3] Andrews. *History of New Britain.* p. 184, Hartford.
[4] Brooks. *Flowering of New England.* p. 248, New York. 1936.

And revivifying that tradition throughout her youth was her father who, following his retirement from military service at the age of thirty-five, employed himself at home in collecting, editing and publishing the twenty folio volumes of the works of Orestes, followed by a two thousand page biography in three large volumes. Since this enormous mass of source material is still available to anyone interested, there is no need to review either his life or his works here.[5] But of course it is important to our purpose to note the determining influences of Orestes Brownson upon his grand-daughter Josephine. The paramount one, of course, was his restoring the ancient Faith to his family through his conversion to Catholicism in 1844. Further, his energy, his lucidity and his facility in languages he passed on to his son Henry who in turn delivered them intact to his daughter Josephine. They were qualities which stood her in good stead, for she used them wisely and well. Yes, even the last mentioned of them, and seemingly the least; for it became the one which, as we shall see, proved to be the key which unlocked a door to her uniquely fruitful career.

To the literary labors of Major Brownson which we have mentioned should be added his translations from the Italian of Tarducci the biographies of John and Sebastian Cabot, and of their even more celebrated countryman and contemporary, Christopher Columbus. It is significant that the translator believed in the sanctity of Columbus and hoped to live to see him canonized.

As indicated, the Major's service to letters followed his retirement from service in the Army. In 1861, he had been commissioned a first lieutenant in the Fifteenth New York Volunteer Engineers, but resigned the following January to

[5] For these and later writings on Orestes A. Brownson see bibliography at the end of this book.

accept appointment in the Regular Army, as a second lieutenant, Third United States Artillery. He was brevetted captain in 1862 and major in 1863 "for gallant and meritorious services" in the Battles of Malvern Hill and Chancellorsville, respectively.[6]

After the war he was a member of the Forty-Third Infantry, stationed at Fort Wayne, near Detroit. His rank, his dignified bearing and his cultured background gave him entree into the rising young city's best family circles. It was thus that he met and courted and married the second daughter of James Adams and Elizabeth (Desnoyers) Van Dyke.

That formal military wedding, celebrated in old St. Anne's, the mother church of the City of the Straits, completed the triptych of racial strains—English, French, Dutch —that went into the making of Josephine Brownson.

Let us here take a brief glance at the backgrounds of the other two families, the Desnoyers and the Van Dykes.

First, the Desnoyers. They were Catholics, and they were silversmiths. Indeed, they were by royal appointment "Silversmiths to the Bourbons."[7] But the terrorists of the French Revolution had slight respect for either religion or royalty. So the head of the house of Desnoyers decided to achieve the safety of his son, and the perpetuation of his name, by arranging for his security in the land of the free, —the land which his beloved France had so recently sent her own sons to help make free. To this end, Desnoyers now purchased in Paris stock in the Scioto Land Company and in 1790 bade adieu to his eighteen year old son and heir, Pierre Jean, that he should go and prosper in America.

The sea voyage of sixty days finally terminated at

[6] Spaulding. Committee on Military Affairs. 47th Congress Report #478.

[7] Desnoyers, in *Biographie Universelle*.

Havre de Grace in Maryland. Then followed an arduous overland journey to the promised (and paid for) land: the present Gallipolis, Ohio. It was not another Paris. There were forests to be cleared, logs to be hewn, cabins to be built, crops to be planted, wells to be dug, and a score of other pioneer tasks to be done. The backwoods of Southeastern Ohio, just across the Virginia frontiers, were not prepared to receive gentlemen from France in 1791. "The colony did not prosper, but its breaking up spread through America a superior type of French Catholic." [8]

Undaunted, young Pierre Jean joined General Anthony Wayne's army en route to the Northwest Territory. There his services as armorer were requisitioned by the government. His commission was signed by General Francis Hamtramck, whose name is perpetuated by a city completely encircled by present-day Detroit.

Following the conclusion of his term of military service in 1803, Pierre Jean returned to Detroit, for its people were his compatriots, retaining their French language and culture. Too, as General Wayne observed, there were "among them a number of wealthy and well-bred merchants and gentlemen and fashionable well-bred women." [9] A prospective clientele for a young man bent upon establishing a successful silversmith shop. But surely Pierre Jean's first reason for returning was to resume his courtship with Marie Louise Gobeille.

They were married and Pierre Jean prospered, "becoming an honorable figure in Detroit history." [10] His silversmithing was interrupted temporarily by the conflagration

[8] Paré. *Catholic Church in Detroit.* f p. 278, Detroit. 1951.
[9] Letter to his son, quoted by F. Cleve Bald. *A Portrait of Anthony Wayne.* Clements Library, Ann Arbor. 1948.
[10] Paré. *op. cit.* p. 278.

of 1805 and again by his commission in Sibley's militia in the War of 1812.

The Desnoyers were not only parishioners of the great Père Gabriel Richard; he was a close personal friend of the family.[11]

Pierre Jean retired from business in 1835 to devote his full time to civic interests. In this too he was successful. He held in turn the office of County Court Judge, United States Marshall for Michigan, and State Treasurer. He was also a member of the first Board of Trustees of the University of Michigan.

Memorable too was the year 1835 for him (and for this memoir) in that during it he gave his elder daughter Elizabeth in marriage to James Adams Van Dyke.[12] They were destined to become parents of Josephine Brownson's mother.

Examples of the artistic craftsmanship of Pierre Jean Desnoyers survive in heirlooms of silver in private collections as well as in the collection of the Detroit Institute of Arts. To him Josephine owed the imaginative feeling and the sureness of line with which she so effectively illustrated several of her own books. And they were books in which the drawings were co-workers with the text in emphasis and clarity, and in explanation of her vital message.

With the Desnoyers–Van Dyke nuptials we are brought to the last of the threefold racial strains in Josephine's ancestry,—the Dutch.

Young James could trace his family roots to Rotterdam

[11] Hickey. *Ste. Anne's Parish:* 100 Years of Detroit History. Wayne University Press, Detroit. 1951.

[12] The younger of Desnoyers' two daughters, Josephine, married the Hartford educator, Henry Barnard, who later founded the Bureau of Education, at Washington, D. C.

whence Achias Janse Van Dyke and his wife Janitse had sailed to Maryland early in the nineteenth century.

Born in 1813, James had been privately tutored until he was sixteen, had graduated from Madison College when he was nineteen, and then proceeded to study law under the Honorable William Price, of Hagerstown, Maryland.

When he came to Detroit to begin practice in 1835, he brought with him a letter of recommendation "both as an attorney and as a gentleman." The letter was addressed to Alexander D. Fraser, President of the Detroit Bar, and was signed by the Honorable Robert McClelland, United States Secretary of the Interior.

Their faith in the twenty-two year old barrister proved amply justified. Attorney for the City from 1835 to 1839, he later served as County Prosecuting Attorney. National recognition came to him when, as Fire Commissioner, he reorganized and modernized the department, and as Mayor in 1847 when he rescued the city from heavy indebtedness. His civic career was equalled in brilliance by his legal and forensic reputation as attorney for the Michigan Central Railroad.

An engraved silver cup, now a proud possession of one of his grandsons, reveals another facet of his character. It was presented to him in 1843 by the Colored citizens of the city out of gratitude to him for defending their delegate who had been barred from a convention held to determine the social and political status of the Negro in Detroit. Such an action today could be political expediency in a city in which every fourth citizen is Colored, many in professional or executive positions; but it was courage in the cause of justice in Van Dyke's day, for nearly all the few Negroes in Detroit then were unskilled laborers or menials.

Shortly before his death in 1855, he was received into

the Church at old St. Anne's. In his Last Will and Testament he proudly asserted: "I, James Adams Van Dyke, am a member of the Roman Catholic Church."

It was as a welcome guest in the Van Dyke home at 308 East Jefferson avenue that Major Henry Francis Brownson wooed and won their daughter Josephine. With their marriage, the three families whose background we have briefly traced, became one. And their daughter, Josephine Van Dyke Brownson, whose life and labors it is our primary purpose to follow intimately, was not English or French or Dutch. She was an American. And she was destined to exemplify and indeed sublimate the fine talents and traits of her threefold heritage.

CHAPTER TWO

"From First Beginnings"

MAJOR BROWNSON AND HIS YOUNG BRIDE EXCHANGED vows in St. Anne's Church in January of 1868. Immediately after the wedding breakfast in the home of the bride's mother the couple left for Atlanta, Georgia. It was not a voluntarily planned honeymoon but strict obedience in line of duty which sent him there. He had been assigned to serve for a year in the Bureau of Refugees, Freedmen and Abandoned Lands, with headquarters in Atlanta. The misery and want left in the wake of Sherman's devastating "March to the Sea" were still so severe that the Brownsons were glad to get back to Fort Wayne, especially since they were expecting their first child. They returned in January of 1869, and Philip James Van Dyke Brownson was born the following May.

When in 1870 the Major was assigned to the Twenty Fifth Infantry and ordered to active duty in Texas, both he and his wife were reluctant to accept the distant assignment, and decided that he should resign from the army.

Previous to his career in the service he had been schooled at Holy Cross College and at Georgetown University, with post-graduate studies in France and Germany. His profession was law, and upon leaving the army he entered into a partnership with his brother-in-law, Philip Van Dyke.

After a year it was dissolved by the death of the junior
partner and Henry discontinued practice entirely to devote
himself to collecting, editing and publishing the scattered
and voluminous writings of his father.

Another pertinent interest of his during this period was
in a Catholic Lay Congress for the United States, such as
had proven so advantageous for the Church in Europe. This
major form of the Catholic Action of his day suited the
breadth of his interests. It also indicates the permeation of
the Faith in the home life of the Brownson family.

By the year 1875, that family included five children.
Following Philip, it had been blest by the births of Sally,
Orestes, Edward, and Ernest. And in October of that year,
their father returned from a visit with his sister Sara, bring-
ing their grandfather Orestes to share their home on High
Street at Second Avenue.

After the death of his wife Sally in April of 1872,
Orestes had made his home with his only daughter, Sara.[13]
A literary luminary in her own right was this same Sara M.
Brownson (1839–1876). By her articles, stories and poems in
her father's *Review*, in *The Catholic World*, and other
periodicals, as well as by her novels, but above all by her
biography of the Russian prince and later missionary priest
in pioneer Pennsylvania, *Demetrius Gallitzin* (1873), she
has merited the distinction of an individual biographical
entry (written by her brother Henry) in *The Catholic Encyclopedia*.[14] After her marriage to William J. Tenney, of Elizabeth, New Jersey, in 1873,[15] she continued to care for her

[13] A brother of Sara and Henry was killed in the Civil War, and her
memorial poem, "A War Litany," was deemed worthy of reprinting some
forty years later. *Cf.* The Catholic World, 102:68–69, Oct. 1915.

[14] Vol. 3, p. 3. New York. 1908–1913.

[15] A daughter by this marriage became Mother Sara Tenney, of the
Religious of the Sacred Heart.

64- 240

father until that same brother Henry came to bring the age-ing sire back to Detroit.

Orestes' only previous stay in Michigan had been more than a half century earlier. In 1824 he had come to teach school in Springwells (then a suburb, now a part of the city of Detroit). But after a severe bout with River Rouge fever and ague, he had returned East the following year.

Brief, too, his second stay. The great man's days with his beloved grandchildren were destined to be few. With the advent of Spring his health failed rapidly and, fortified by the Sacraments of the Church he had served so coura-geously and so ably, he passed into his eternal reward on Easter Monday, 1876.

Ten years after his burial in the family plot in Mount Elliott Cemetery, Detroit, his remains were transferred to a crypt beneath an extension of Sacred Heart Church, known as the Brownson Memorial Chapel, on the campus of the University of Notre Dame.

But between the burial and the reburial of Orestes, two births took place in the family of his son Henry, one of them the subject of this biography.

In 1879, after the birth of Elizabeth, their sixth child, the Brownsons moved into their newly built home at 243 East Larned Street. And there Josephine Van Dyke Brown-son was born on January 26, 1880. It was the feast of St. Polycarp, whose name signifies "abundant fruit." Two days later, the infant was baptized by her uncle, the Reverend Ernest Van Dyke, in St. Anne's Church.[16] The pastor, the

[16] Builder of the present St. Mary's Church in Adrian, Father Van Dyke had been transferred to the Cathedral in Detroit. He died as pastor of St. Aloysius Church, Detroit. A Domestic Prelate, he is remembered as Monsignor Van Dyke.

In 1880, St. Anne's was located across the street from the Brownson residence, on the square bounded by Larned, Bates, Congress and Randolph streets; six years later it was demolished and rebuilt on its present location, about a mile to the west. Paré. *op. cit.* p. 545.

Reverend Theophilus Anceaux, an old friend of the family, was one of the sponsors; the other was Emily V. Barnard, a first cousin of the tiny new Christian.

One familiar with the tense pace and the exhaust fumes, the ugliness and the noise of 243 East Larned and vicinity today needs to have recalled to mind the neighborhood as it was in 1880, when the present city of nearly three million was a leisurely town of a hundred and sixteen thousand souls. Stately elms lined both sides of Larned then, their branches meeting overhead and casting shadows on the cobblestone road. The chirping of birds, the chatter of children at play and the rhythm of horse-drawn carriages occasionally varied the placid scene. The residences were well spaced and bordered by flower gardens, while to the rear were fruit trees and flowering shrubs. In this setting stood the Brownson home. A red brick, gray stone trimmed colonial, with broad steps leading up to its full width veranda. And within were the high ceilings of the period, the polished wing-doors of dark inlaid wood, the wainscoted dining room, and open fire places in library, sitting and drawing rooms.

In this gracious and spacious atmosphere Josephine spent her childhood. As the youngest of seven children, she, unawares but of necessity, learned early the art of living with others with its lessons of give and take and share. Thus she was afforded the opportunities and advantages of the present day pre-school. Until she was eight her formal lessons too were learned at home. Her mother grounded her in the fundamentals of the catechism, in the rudiments of reading, writing and arithmetic.

In September of 1888, she was enrolled in the day school of the Academy of the Sacred Heart, then located on Jefferson avenue, across the street from SS. Peter and Paul Jesuit Church. She retained a life-long affection for Mother Matilda Sullivan, R.S.C.J., her first teacher.

Happy too were the pupil friendships of those first years. Winifred Corbett, Bertha Stott and Lizzie Fleitz who were sharing her play and study world were to share her world of memories.

Significant is an item taken from her sixth grade record. It testifies that Josephine not only wore the Pink Ribbon good conduct award that year but that she took her religion classes with the grade ahead of her. But for her that year of 1890 was memorable for two still more important reasons. Following a three day Retreat, which ended on Ascension Thursday, May fifteenth, little Josephine and twelve of her companions received their First Holy Communion and were confirmed. Both Sacraments were administered in the Academy chapel by the Right Reverend John Samuel Foley, Bishop of Detroit.

In her second year of high school the record reveals that Latin had been added to her course, but it is doctrine again that it underscores. She received a perfect mark and thus the doctrine medal.

The bonds of the family were first broken in that year of 1894. Philip went to sea, Sally entered the novitiate of the Religious of the Sacred Heart at Kenwood, Elizabeth became resident pupil at the nuns' Grosse Pointe academy, and Grandmother Van Dyke died.

The next year Josephine joined Elizabeth, and the year following, Sally; though of course not as a postulant but as an academy pupil.

During the summer vacation, on August 26, 1896, to be exact, Josephine for the first time became a member of an organization. Due to her life-long singleness of purpose and her ever-crowded days, there were to be few, very few, that she would join. But to them, as to this first, she would give a life-time of loyalty. It was at the City House of the

Academy that her name was inscribed as a new member of the confraternity of the Apostleship of Prayer. Its national director, Father John J. Wynne, S.J., signed her certificate. Twenty two years later he was to sign his Preface to her first book.

Josephine attended Kenwood (Albany, New York) for her high school graduation year. And from two mementos we can see the girl who was mother to the woman.

The first is a fifty-page story, written with a firm, round hand, in a drab, brown, six by nine notebook. Its title-page reads: The Martyr of the Cross // by J. Brownson // To my sincere friend Marie Ross // this book is Affectionately Ascribed // First Edition // Kenwood, N. Y. // 1897

It is the story of a girl whom a good teacher so interests in the lessons of the catechism that she refines her own life and reforms those of her brother and parents, and eventually becomes a foreign missionary nun who is beaten to death by infidels for her refusal to deny the Faith.

Grammatically flawless, in prose more dignified than cadenced, the story reads smoothly to its dramatic climax. However, it reveals not so much a rather immature novelist as a rather mature catechist. The sequence of this seventeen year old girl's narrative is the one she will use all her life: engender interest, which will lead to love, and result in spiritualized thinking and living.

Nor can the years increase or improve upon her realization of the sublimity of the vocation she is choosing. "O glorious mission, little Apostle, to bring back souls to the Feet of Jesus and open for them the Gates of Paradise!" Her salutation to the heroine of her story was, in the Providence of God, to her future self.

A responsive chord in her soul must have been struck early by the Religious of the Sacred Heart as well as a firm foundation laid. For, three years before this, she had offered her services to Father J. V. Geerts, pastor of the little Belgian parish of Our Lady of Sorrows, to prepare his First Communicants. How convinced he soon became of her competence is revealed by a simple but striking incident. When she had finished giving the course, she invited him to be present for the final review. At its conclusion she turned and asked his verdict. The over-tired old shepherd, roused from his nap with a start, stated simply: "If you say they are prepared, Miss Josephine, I know they are."

We are also privileged to see her at seventeen through the eyes of her classmates, for one of them has left us a candid portrait. Cornelia Craigie, who assisted the managing editor of *The Catholic Encyclopedia* and later wrote a biographical dictionary of its collaborators, was her classmate at Kenwood.

"Josephine was a great favorite in the school," writes Miss Craigie. "Everyone liked her, many exceedingly. She was athletic, in spite of a back that tired easily. She had the finest mind in the school by long odds, and was only amused at our astonishment when we saw her reading the *Summa* for diversion. She was entirely unconventional, large-minded and high-spirited."

When Josephine graduated from high school at Kenwood in 1897, she returned to her home in Detroit and enrolled for special courses in Central High School. Then she earned a diploma from the Detroit Normal Training School, for she intended to become a teacher.

While attending these two schools she was an active member of the Sacred Heart Alumnae. Fortunately for our information, this group then drew the speakers for its meetings from its own membership, rather than invited guests. Thus we are afforded a reflection of her academic interests and her home atmosphere, but not of her heart, between the ages of eighteen and twenty-two. Remembering that the members were free to select their own topics, much is revealed by the mere listing of Josephine's. "Literary Women of France and Germany," December, 1899; "Russia's Internal Policy," March, 1901; "Girls of Today and Yesterday," April, 1901; "English Drama," February, 1902; "Great Men of England," April, 1902.

These titles might have been selected from one of the twenty tomes of her grandfather Orestes or from the nearly equally voluminous writings of her father Henry. As has been indicated, the Brownson tradition must have exerted a powerful influence upon the mind of Josephine. It should not be lost sight of that it was at home that her father produced the twenty three folio volumes of and on Orestes life and works; at home where, with respites few and brief, Josephine lived until her father's death when she was a mature woman of thirty-three. It is interesting, indeed significant, that she herself in her own writing and speaking career, never mentioned the name of Orestes Brownson. That her life revealed hereditary traits we know, and the fact will become increasingly evident. But it happened to be one of those very traits, her strength of will, which now enabled her to free herself from the old Brownson tradition and to create for it a new and quite independent expression. The subjects of the talks she delivered before the Sacred Heart Alumnae between 1899 and 1902 are the last anyone will ever hear of them from her. For in her life and its expression the echo of Orestes and Henry is being succeeded by the voice of Josephine.

This is the end of a definite phase in her life. Though elected a member of the Speakers' Committee of the Alumnae for 1901–1902, she resigned from active membership in October of the latter year. It might be mentioned that she resigned to enter upon her first public school teaching assignment; it must be mentioned that she resigned to devote all her future talks to the apostolate in which she had already apprenticed herself and which she was soon to begin making her destined career. However, she never resigned a loyalty and, regardless of the pressure on her time, to the end of her days she attended her alumnae meetings if only to show her presence, then slip away, back to her work.

Josephine began teaching English at the Barstow Public School in Detroit in 1903, remaining till she went to get her Bachelor of Arts degree from the University of Michigan.[17] Because of her Normal School training, the degree was earned after two years of study, in 1913.

Invaluable as an estimate of her character and ability at this time is a note addressed to the principal of Cass Technical High School. It is dated January 15, 1914; and it reads:

My dear Dr. Chadsey:
A letter from Miss Josephine Brownson informs me of her having received her B.A. last summer, and of her desire to teach in the Cass Technical High. She has not asked me to speak to you of her but, as I am greatly interested in her career, I take the liberty to write you.

She came to the Barstow School directly from the Detroit Normal and was with me there until I was transferred to the Capron School. She is a student: has for some years kept up a correspondence course with the University of Chicago; is honest and earnest in her work; is a lady with the background of a family of education and culture. She has gained her higher education

[17] The University of Detroit was not yet co-educational; and there was not then any Catholic college for women in Michigan.

26

through unusual effort, and deserves encouragement where it is possible. I am confident that you will understand this communication of mine to be prompted by interest in one of "my girls" rather than by any desire to influence your appointment.

                    Most sincerely yours,
                    (signed) H. Jane Cooper [18]

To have merited such a letter of recommendation from so fine a character as this letter reveals Miss Cooper to have been is in itself no small praise.

Josephine was appointed a teacher of mathematics at Cass Technical High School in the Fall of 1914, becoming second assistant in 1919. And so the faith of Miss Cooper in her proved more than justified, and Josephine's new associates could have repeated the letter if an occasion for it had ever arisen.

Completing twenty-five years in the educational system of the City of Detroit in 1928, Josephine retired and devoted the remainder of her life exclusively to the work which had been nearest her heart since she was a child. We have touched upon its first public expression at Our Lady of Sorrows. But we must go back now to follow its formation and development as an organized apostolate.

[18] Original in the files of the Detroit Board of Education.

CHAPTER THREE

The Star and the Child

BECAUSE JOSEPHINE'S CAREER AND THE PHENOMENAL growth of Detroit between 1900 and 1912 were intimately allied, it is important for our purpose for us to understand not only the fact but the nature of that growth. The automobile was, of course, the primary cause of it. Oldsmobiles, Cadillacs and Packards were in production in Detroit and vicinity before Henry Ford entered upon the scene. But their price was around $2,000; the equivalent of about $5,000 in today's purchasing power. Thus confined to the few, their production created but a negligible new labor market. But Ford, tinkering in his back yard workshop on Bagley Street a few short blocks from Josephine's home, envisioned a mass market for a car within its means. To get that market he reduced his automobile to bare essentials and assembled them on a time and money saving conveyor system. The result was the immortal Model T. It retailed for $345, F.O.B. Detroit. By 1927 he had sold more than fifteen million of them.[19]

Such a volume of production so localized created an enormous new labor market, not only to manufacture the parts and to assemble them, but to provide food, clothing, shelter and recreation for the thousands so employed. Mostly unskilled labor responded to the call to tear up roots and

[19] Allan Nevins. *Ford:* the Times, the Man, the Company. New York. 1954.

come to work in a distant city. Unskilled, usually poor of course, and largely foreign born. The sole possessions of many were brought in a sack slung across their backs.

A great many entered the city through the railroad station at down town Fort and Third streets. Across from it stood (and still stands) the Presbyterian Church, then the most fashionable Protestant place of worship in the city. Seeing the church as they left the station, many a job-seeking newcomer approached it for directions, for counsel, for help. Having no place to send them, and unwilling to turn them away, the pastor and people of the Presbyterian Church organized a social service department to help them.

The influx had been so sudden and so great that the city government itself was unprepared for it and had only the quickly overcrowded Franklin Street Settlement.

Due especially to the large number of Italians, Hungarians, Poles and Irish among the new arrivals, they included a good percentage of Catholics. They too, of course, were among those who shared the social service facilities of the Presbyterian Church.[20]

A rather full account of their work in *The Detroit News* snapped Josephine to attention as she browsed through its pages on returning home from her day of teaching.

"They can't have them! They are ours!" she exclaimed to herself. And without a thought of how or where she would attempt the gigantic task of preserving and strengthening the Faith in these rootless children of the Church, she straightway left the room, the house, the street and went to them.

A high school classmate had called her "unconventional, large-minded and high-spirited." In this moment she

[20] *The Story of the Fort Street Presbyterian Church.* Centennial Committee of the Church, Detroit. 1949.

is all of these. Strong willed and of solid piety too. With these she brought a humble but essential key, the gift of languages. For what could she have done if she could not even have made herself understood by them? An Italian group was her first contact. She spoke to them as Catholic to Catholic. She offered to help them get settled, to learn to speak English, to have their children cared for. As a Sacred Heart alumna she trooped them over to her old teachers on Jefferson avenue.

These nuns had conducted a free school for poor children as well as their academy.[21] When the Jesuits took up their work at SS. Peter and Paul Church across the street, the pupils of the free school automatically became the pupils of the parish school. Thus the nuns were left with a vacant building. But not for long. The instantly answered plea of Father Beccherini, Detroit's only Italian pastor in 1903, transformed it into a free school for poor children again.[22] And so it was here that Josephine brought not only her first group but succeeding ones. Here she helped to train and to teach after her own arduous day in a public school classroom. And here she brought the funds she set about raising to help with the heat, the light and the other bills the undertaking incurred.

The gradual solving of this phase of the problem impressed upon her mind another, one which she did not have to go out and seek. For by its nature it was part of her professional life, and by her nature she must do something about it.

While attending the Detroit Normal School, Josephine had had the opportunity of observing how the religious vacuum of a secular institution threatened the Faith of a

[21] Their foundress, St. Madeleine, designated both of these fields of labor for her spiritual daughters.

[22] Louise Callan, R.S.C.J. *The Society of the Sacred Heart in North America*. pp. 464–66, New York. 1937.

Catholic student. It might weaken it; it might even destroy it; but one thing was certain, it was hardly to be expected that it would strengthen it. Yet a student stood at least as much in need of spiritual as of mental development. For good citizenship, to say nothing of good character development, they belong together.

If it had been her problem as a Catholic student in a public school, it became much more her problem as a Catholic teacher in a public school. From the fact that she at once tried to do something about it, it is evident that she recognized that she had an obligation in the matter; and the manner in which she set about to do something about it is evidence of the seriousness with which she regarded that obligation.

To begin with, she considered the question of why in the first place Catholic children were attending the public schools. The answer to that would provide her with an answer to the question of how she could best help him.

While some of them lived too far from the then few parish schools and others could not afford even the low parochial school tuition the majority of them were from families which, largely due to their own lack of religious instruction, were not particularly concerned about it being given their children. As we have observed, the enormous influx of laborers into the city included thousands of Catholic families.

The diocese of Detroit did not have sufficient funds or teachers to immediately meet the situation. So for that reason too great numbers of Catholic children (they were estimated as many as fifty thousand) had no choice but the public school.

But this lack of religious instruction was imperiling their Faith, so much so that if they did not get it, it was unlikely that they would remain practical Catholics. If that statement seems exaggerated, let us recall the words of the future Pope St. Pius X, uttered when he was Father Sarto, pastor of the town of Tombolo. In maintaining that attendance at instructions was even more important than attendance at devotions he asked: "What will the devotions of the Church profit you if you do not understand their meaning? And how can you understand the homilies and sermons if you are ignorant of the primary and most necessary truths?" [23]

That was the apostolate of Josephine Brownson: to instruct in the teachings of their religion Catholic pupils attending public schools. She began alone, gradually enlisting the co-operation of her Catholic confreres in the Detroit public school system. She formulated a teacher-training course in catechetics for them, and trained them in it. She worked out a unique and effective religious instruction course for the particular type of children they were to instruct, and supervised their mastering it, and then their imparting of it to their pupils. She began alone. Through prayer and labor, through wisdom and tact, she so developed her apostolate that in her own lifetime it came to conduct seventy five Catechetical Centers with four hundred and fifty four volunteer teachers and more than fourteen thousand children under instruction at one time.

This acorn to oak development deserves to be traced in some detail.

[23] *Articolo per il processo apostolo del Servo di Dio Pio Papa X.* p. 15, Rome. 1943.

CHAPTER FOUR

Eternal Candle

YEARS AFTER SHE HAD ESTABLISHED THE CATHOLIC INstruction League, Josephine was asked by Father Michael Pathe, C.SS.R., for an account of its beginnings. Humility could have asked little less of her reply; her biographer much more. But, sketchy as it is, it is, of course, invaluable; we have filled in the lacunae as much as possible.

First, she endeavored to discover the Catholic and should-be-Catholic pupils in her public school classroom and gradually in her entire school. From their names, from their nationalities, through discreet questioning, through tips (offered or unconsciously given) by teachers, parents and other pupils, she tactfully but persistently followed the trail until she not only discovered whether these pupils belonged to the Church but also their attitude toward it; and—what was usually the most potent factor—the attitude of their parents toward it. She then set out to gain the confidence of the child by a sincerely sympathetic interest in his studies and in his games, but especially in his other activities, in his hopes and plans for the future. As the number of her proteges increased she formed a little social club for them. They were served sandwiches and ice cream and discussed informally the general ideas of life, vocation, religion, God. For entertainment at the meetings she provided colored slides embodying historical facts of a religious nature and of the lands of the Bible.

Her commentary on them was both interesting and instructive. While she, of course, desired to influence as many pupils as possible, she did not want the group to become so large as to weaken that influence. Hence, as the numbers in attendance increased, she divided them by age levels into separate groups and held their meetings on different days.

It is a particular gift, that of influencing the young in such a way that they trust you, confide in you; that they seek and follow your guidance. Not all teachers have it, nor even all parents. Josephine was blest with this gift in a superlative degree. Not only do all who knew her testify to the fact, but her whole career proves it. She developed these individual contacts so successfully that the number of children receiving religious instruction during a single school year from her and her associates, whom she had trained, came to exceed fourteen thousand.

She was convinced even at that early date, of what today is a well-publicized fact, that to save the child one must save the home; that the moral breakdown of the home would be the disaster of the nation. And her ability here was equally notable. Typical is this incident reported by Mary K. Kirby, one of her associate teachers:

"Having failed completely, after several attempts, to get into the home of a pupil about to be Confirmed and unable to produce a Baptismal Certificate, I called Josephine to the rescue. She not only got into the home but before long had the mother coming back to church, had the father listening to her, arranged a daughter's marriage to be rectified, grandchildren baptized, a son taking instructions, and my little pupil provided with a certificate. You see why the Holy Ghost hadn't let me in!"

The little informal groups that Josephine began first to organize became too numerous for her to handle alone and in her home; so she enlisted the assistance of her fellow Catholic public school teachers and sought for an adequate meeting place. Thus it came about in 1906 that she secured permission from Father James J. Foley, S.J., to use the basement rooms of SS. Peter and Paul School. There Josephine and her fellow teachers began to gather their Catholic pupils on Friday afternoons. "The object," she recorded, "was not to recite catechism but to interest them in their religion and make them understand it by intelligent talks."

Particularly in the words "interest" and "understand" we have, as we shall see, a foreshadowing of her religious instruction teaching technique. So too her reference to the catechism; that will come to cause a great deal of unnecessary misunderstanding.

These Friday afternoon sessions became popular, their attendance reaching ninety within a few weeks. But after a year the rooms were needed by the school, and Josephine had to find another location. That comes to have a familiar ring too!

This was not easy. Schools were hard put for space rather than having any to spare. Rented quarters were out of the question, for the undertaking had no financial backing. In her need Josephine turned to her personal friends. She asked Mrs. Francis Palms for the use of the sixty-foot carriage house on the Palms Estate at 500 East Jefferson avenue. The request was graciously granted. More friends then brought hammer and nails, brushes and paint, and soon had the premises remodeled; others donated equipment and supplies; the Detroit Public Library put a subbranch in the hayloft; and George L. Fleitz completed the layout with a billiard table.

"We carried on for about four years in the barn. Monday afternoons were for boys under twelve; Tuesday for boys of twelve and over. One night a week was for working girls and another for working boys. Each meeting started with prayers and an instruction. Only those present for the instruction could take part in the activities that followed. We had sewing classes, bowling teams, boxing, billiards, stunts on a horse, etc."

George Reno, a University of Detroit student who became a Jesuit priest, had charge of the gym class. Speaking of Jesuits, they were from the beginning generous and enthusiastic co-operators: Fathers Edward Sullivan, Richard Slevin, Michael Stritch, Michael Gorman, as well as several of their scholastics. Her lay friends in the initial foundation included Winifred Corbett (Mrs. Harold Palmer), Florence Knill (Mrs. Maurice Quinn), Elizabeth and Laura McPherson, Amelia McSweeney, Alice Ward, Marie Leslie Seymour and Alice Chapoton. Nor were the men wanting who were needed to visit homes, teach the older boys, and otherwise serve the cause. Among the pioneers must be mentioned Raymond Cameron, Eugene Paulus, and Marius Risley.[24]

In 1911 and 1912, summer playgrounds were added to the activities of the group; one on the east and another on the west side of the city.

Strange as it seems, all these undertakings had been launched and had progressed anonymously. Yet, not so strange, for Josephine always labored to win souls, not a reputation. But now a name was needed to identify the group in matters of purchases and supplies and other transactions. In honor of their principal adviser, Father Henry Weinman, S.J., the name decided upon was the Weinman Club. It was at this time too that increasing attendance

[24] Mr. Cameron, an attorney, has devoted his life to the practice of charity rather than of the law. In 1949, Mr. Paulus was received into the Oblates of St. Francis de Sales, and professed the following July. Mr. Risley became a professor in a Catholic college in Buffalo, N. Y.

necessitated their moving from the Palms barn to larger quarters.

The social service department of the Club was becoming more and more its predominant activity. Josephine had not begun it for that purpose but for the imparting of religious instruction. Any other activities were to her but means to that end. But both types of work were needed and neither should be curtailed, much less discontinued. And so in 1916, she urged a division of the work and of the workers. This resulted in the formation of the League of Catholic Women, under the presidency of Mrs. Herman Dey, succeeded soon by Mrs. Wilfred Casgrain; and the Catholic Instruction League, under the direction of Josephine. The name of her group was suggested by Father John M. Lyons, S.J. The League of Catholic Women continued the social work program and under it the Weinman Club became the Weinman Settlement.

The Catholic Instruction League soon became familiarly known as the C.I.L., and thus more often than not we will henceforth refer to it.

Under Josephine's inspiration and guidance it developed steadily, increasing in the number of its instruction Centers, in the size of the teaching staff which she continued to recruit largely from her fellow public school teachers, and in the multitude of its pupils. But behind that simple statement of fact lay self-sacrifice and apostolic zeal. It should be remembered that, as with Josephine herself, most of the C.I.L. teachers were otherwise employed full time. They gave up their after hours, their days off, their evenings when they might have relaxed at home, or entertained, or gone to a musicale or the theatre. Instead, it was then that they visited homes to get parents' permission for their children to take religious instruction courses; then that they roamed the streets in search of strays; then that they rode street cars or busses to whatever church or school or home or hall or basement or even field that they could get to teach in. These small, scattered and uncertain locations made it as difficult to get the pupils together as it was for the teachers to get to them. This lack of suitable and sufficient teaching quarters was threatening the existence of the C.I.L., to say nothing of hampering its growth. It was accommodated inadequately; it was getting too big to be accommodated at all.

"A religious school must be patterned after a regular school," declared Josephine. "It must have professional teachers, and a principal. Classes must be held in classrooms, not in basements, gymnasiums, or hallways."

To solve the problem she decided on a bold stroke. Happily, we have her own account of it.

"A Protestant minister, in several articles in a Detroit newspaper, attacked the public schools because of their irreligious atmosphere. I called upon him and suggested that the Catholic and Protestant groups provide teachers for a supplementary course in religion to be taught right in the public schools. We soon found that the Jewish group was also willing to take part. The combined group then requested consideration from the Detroit Board of Education. We got one day a week set aside for instructions which were to be given in a period following the close of the regular session." [25]

The permission included the reservation that the teachers would not conduct their religious instruction classes in the same schools to which they were assigned by the Board of Education. Under this arrangement, the C.I.L. teachers were left with the necessity of rushing from their

[25] The year was 1932. It was thus due to Josephine's initiative that non-Catholic children in the Detroit public schools were likewise enabled to receive instruction in their own religious beliefs under these advantageous conditions.

public school classes to another location for their religion class assignments. But at least it was to another public school building rather than to makeshift teaching quarters. Aside from that one restriction (and that disadvantageous to the teachers but not to the pupils), the new arrangement was completely on the credit side of the ledger. The pupils had only to be kept together instead of having to be brought together; and the C.I.L. now had ample and fitting teaching accommodations. And would continue to have them; for the city would build new schools to keep pace with the increase of pupil population.

Encouraged by her success with the City, Josephine sought and obtained permission for the C.I.L. to give religious instruction to the children of the Wayne County Training School for Subnormals at Northville,[26] the Michigan Convalescent Home for Children at Farmington, the Detroit Detention Home, and eventually the Public Schools of the City of Hamtramck.

All this expansion meant more teachers for Josephine to recruit and then to train for the work, more classes for her to supervise, more assignment schedules, more demonstration lessons, more substituting by herself for absent teachers, and more individual pupil's problems to be analyzed and solved.

Add to this her own family responsibilities. To get her Master's degree she had returned to the University of Michigan in October of 1913, but her father's illness quickly brought her home again. He died shortly before Christmas of that year.

Josephine was a mature woman of nearly thirty-four when her father died. For more than thirty of those years

[26] The C.I.L. began giving instructions at Northville in 1921; and in 1929 Father (now Rt. Rev. Msgr.) Edward J. Hickey obtained the Sunday Mass permission from the Hospital Board.

they had lived in close family association. Unusually close, for within a year or two of her birth in 1880 until his death late in December of 1913, Henry had worked as well as lived at home. His influence on her must have been very great. What was it? What kind of a man was he? We have already mentioned that after his retirement as a major in the Federal Army he had practiced law briefly and then devoted some twenty years of his life to collecting and editing his father's varied and voluminous works, followed by a bulky three-volume biography. If Henry had sacrificed his own career on the altar of his father, at least he was to be rewarded with the Laetare Medal. But certainly he could not have foreseen that. There is no question of his loyalty to his father's reputation, nor to the fact that he enhanced it, if he did not actually keep it alive. Such loyalty demanded intense devotion. That devotion must have been a monotonous dish on the family table. But with the growth of the children the monologues developed into dialogues, and tolerance was learned and practiced. He was strict; in her charity, his quiet, gentle wife would have denied that he was domineering. His military bearing was an external expression of his mind,—formal, precise, thorough. The "oldest citizen" remembers him wearing his military cape; recalls how he rose to leave the moment the priest finished saying Mass, his family striving to keep up with him as he marched down the aisle, the congregation wondering what it was like at home. . . . The Major (as he wanted to be addressed) had something like a sense of humor, loved good company and settled philosophical and theological problems for them. Especially in his later years, he was known to relish his status as a gentleman of leisure. Without question, he loved his family and, within his means, took good care of them. The means came largely from his wife's people. The Van Dykes were well to do. It was Grandmother Van Dyke who financed Henry's seven-foot book-shelf of Orestes.

Josephine reacted quietly but clearly against the Brownson legend and the Van Dyke legacy. Her mind began early to prepare her when the time came to create her own career and to do so independently. She took a within-her-means correspondence course until she was able, from her savings as a teacher in the Barstow School, to go to the University of Michigan for her Bachelor's degree. Following her father's death, she resumed her studies for her Master's at Ann Arbor in January of 1914, but a severe attack of pneumonia the following May sent her home again. Her recovery was not considered satisfactory, and she was sent to a sanitarium in Battle Creek for six weeks. She was never able to resume her university course.

In the spring of 1917, two of her brothers, Orestes and Ernest, died within seven weeks of each other. Orestes had been more or less an invalid most of his life. Although his recovery was not expected, neither was his early death. In fact, Josephine had often voiced the hope that they would share their old age together. The death of Orestes too was unexpected; he died suddenly following an emergency operation.

Her sister Sara had, of course, remained a member of the Religious of the Sacred Heart. When the nuns developed Manhattanville from an academy into a college in 1917, she was one of its organizers and was appointed its first dean.

Between the demands on her time by her home and school and the C.I.L., Josephine had hardly an hour she could call her own. For years she followed an almost split-second routine. Early morning rising; daily Mass and Communion; a full teaching schedule in a public school classroom, broken at noon by lunch and a visit to the Blessed

41

Sacrament; active C.I.L. work until shortly before dinner when she usually took her mother out for a drive, often around Belle Isle or along the shore of Lake St. Clair; and in the evening, either meetings or the writing of books, articles, lectures, correspondence.

Some idea of the increasing magnitude of her labors may be illustrated by these typical statistics:

1929	60 Centers	375 Teachers	11,923 Pupils
1934	62 Centers	400 Teachers	12,200 Pupils
1938	74 Centers	454 Teachers	14,132 Pupils

But the zeal of Josephine and her associates is not fully indicated, even statistically, by those figures. Glancing over the meager and scattered records available we find entries such as these:

For the year 1929, the C.I.L. report includes as addenda: 17 children baptized; 2,626 prepared for First Communion; 207 placed in parochial schools; 6 marriages validated; 24 adult conversions; and 26 adults brought back to the practice of their religion.

And for the year 1936: 2,300 First Communions; 120 children baptized; 210 children placed in Catholic schools; 8 marriages validated; 39 adult converts; 48 adults returned to the practice of the Faith; 400 staff teachers and 13,512 children under instruction.[27]

If it could be had, anything like a full report, even in bare statistical form, would require a volume in itself. Remember, her work spanned some thirty-five years! But surely enough has been given here to enable the reader to form some estimate of the nature and the extent of Josephine's apostolate through her Catholic Instruction League.

[27] M. L. Seymour. *Journal of the Associated Alumnae of the Sacred Heart.* p. 66, Oct. 1937.

CHAPTER FIVE

"Their young eyes grew sudden fair
With dawning answers there"

FOR AN EXPLANATION OF HER CATECHETICAL METHOD, WE
can not be expected to improve upon the one given by Josephine herself; and then for a critical appraisal of it, we are
fortunate in having the verdict of another expert. These are
given without comment, for none is needed.

First, Josephine:

If we tell a child the story of Little Red Riding Hood
or of Jack the Giant Killer, he unconsciously learns the story
and loves it and asks to hear it over and over again. We pay
no attention to motivations, to reactions, to devices and a
hundred other things. We do not exhaust the child to make
sure he knows the story. We do not ply him with questions
about the wolf, the grandmother, Jack or the giant. The child
is so interested that spontaneously he asks us questions and
clears up his own difficulties as far as they can be cleared.

Religion is a story. It is the most fascinating story in the
world. It is one that child and adult instinctively love. The
child is made for God. We do not need to drill religion into
him. He takes to it as a duck takes to water. The child by nature loves religion. He eats it up, he drinks it in. We are the
ones who poison religion for him. We give it to him as though
it were bad medicine that will do him good only if we can

get him to gulp it down. We use the catechism as a wedge to separate him from God. The first thing we tell him about God is that He is a spirit infinitely perfect. Isn't that enough to put a bad taste in his mouth?

We leave the fountain of living water and dig for ourselves broken cisterns that can hold no water. Because the teaching of religion is so easy and so delightful and commands such a wealth of material, we perversely try to make it knotty.

The hour of religion might well be called The True Story Hour. "But," some will object, "you leave nothing to study." What of it? Our food doesn't nourish us if we are conscious of the process of digestion. The hour of religion is an hour of undiluted joy. If you teach mathematics or English or music, some of your pupils have a natural love for the subject, but the majority have not. You think: If all of them loved it, what a paradise the class would be! Let me present you with a paradise. Here it is. The religion class! For every pupil loves it. He is made for it and fits into it as a key into the lock for which it is made.

A child goes to a movie that stirs him. He loves it. Unconsciously he goes home and acts portions of it. A child listens to our religious instruction. He loves it and goes away and starts practicing real virtues. If he loves the hour of religion, he will love the Church and the Sacraments, and that love will bind him to them. And he can't fail to love it, if we don't spoil it.

One of our teachers told the story of the Fall of the Angels. A little girl was so enthusiastic about it that she went home and wrote the story out and presented it to the teacher in an envelope. Another teacher recently told me that she and her class are so fascinated with the story of Adam and Eve and that there is so much to tell about them that it seems as though they'll never get any further, and she herself is spending her days walking through the Garden. The pupils of these teachers will never need to be drilled about the first sin, the creation of hell, who the devils are, Adam and Eve, original sin, the consequences of sin, the promise of a Redeemer.

The dean of a Catholic college, which has the reputation of being the finest girls' college in the east, told me she believed the devil never rejoiced more than over the Bible histories which have prevailed in our schools. They are frightfully illustrated, dry as dust, written by accurate theologians who have manfully crushed every trace of heart and imagination.[28]

I found a boy of fourteen who knew nothing of religion, although he had been baptized a Catholic. He was a working boy, and I instructed him. When I gave him a little New Testament, he read it every day at his noon-hour. He was very shy but one day he managed to say, "If I had only known that religion was like this, I'd have come before."

The catechism is as necessary as the dictionary. It makes for accuracy. We do not hand a teacher a dictionary and tell her to teach English. Neither should we hand a teacher a catechism and tell her to teach religion. Such methods work disaster. The catechism is an epitome, a summary. It is uninteresting but useful to nail down and hold in place doctrines explained in instructions and stories that have *already* been given.

Nothing is more delightful from a teaching standpoint than to come across a boy or girl of thirteen or fourteen years of age who knows nothing whatever of religion. He has not been turned against religion by poor teaching. His mind has

[28] Great strides have been made in their style and format since this was written. Josephine's influence had much to do with that, as we shall see.

45

not been numbed and calloused by constant hammerings with a catechism. Of course, the tiny child is still unspoiled as well.

It is first impressions that are deepest and most lasting. Let a child get his first impressions on some subject from the dry definitions of the catechism and you will never be able to rid him of these poor, inadequate impressions.

When I had my first lessons in geography, I faced the south. According to the map, I was "headed" north, with the east to my right and the west to my left. I have never been able to correct that first impression. I am quite capable of finding the points of the compass, but if you were to ask me in what direction the Atlantic Ocean lies, *instinctively* I'd point to the west. My imagination will always picture it there.

I have in mind a teacher who, in giving a class their first lesson on the Crucifixion, said in a monotonous tone, totally wanting in reverence and love: "Our Lord died on a cross between two thieves." The impression she gave was repellant, almost blasphemous. In contrast is a teacher who told the children in a voice saturated with love and with tears in her own eyes, how the nails pierced our dear Lord's tender hands and feet, how the thorns of the terrible crown were pressed deep into His dear head. The first class were untouched and restless. The second class were spell-bound, the tears ran down their little cheeks. The story of its own weight had taught them love for God and sorrow for sin. The sight of the crucifix will mean little to the first class; it will *always* rouse love and sorrow in the second class.

And so my point is that religion should be taught as a story and presented dramatically. Our Lord did not go about catechising like Socrates. He asked questions here and there by way of bringing out great points or clearing up a difficulty. But for the most part He told stories.

Our teachers themselves have been poorly taught and it is difficult to tear them away from the catechism. They gravitate towards it. It gives them something definite to do, and saved them the trouble of thinking. We must wrest it from them and get them to use it as a trailer *after* the presentation of a given story, as a hammer to drive strengthening nails into the beautiful structure we have raised.

But not all our teachers are thoroughly grounded in religion and not all of them are enthusiastic. Outlines are useless except for the pleasure they afford the one who makes them. Teachers incapable of making their own outlines, are incapable of filling them out.

"Tell us about the angels" or "Tell us the story of Adam and Eve," says the outline. Very good. But *how* will that story be told? Had the story of Little Red Riding Hood been written in some such style as the following, no child would have asked to hear it a second time. "Once there was an immature creature composed of body and soul and clothed in scarlet. Her maternal parent commissioned her to carry various foodstuffs to her own maternal parent who was suffering from a grevious malady. On her course through an arboreal grove, she was intercepted by a quadruped of the lupine family. Etc."

The author of Little Red Riding Hood knew how to tell a story to children and through all the generations that story has been told and read to children, the tellers and the readers have caught its spirit. So must our books of instruction be written by one who understands telling stories to children, and our teachers will catch their spirit.

We must put into the hands of our teachers the stories

they are to tell, exactly as they are to tell them. Of course, as they gain experience, they will elaborate the stories in their own characteristic style.

There should, in general, be no separate classes for catechism, for bible history, for church history. Dogma and history should be intimately blended. In the heart of every story should be a dogma or point of doctrine or morals. Dogmas are not dry things. It is their definitions that are dry.

In Detroit we have the problem of reaching "the other half," the problem that exists throughout the country. We are trying to instruct our children who do not attend Catholic schools, by holding classes one hour a week. A teacher is given a little pamphlet [*Stopping the Leak*] to study. In it is the schedule followed by all classes and a detailed explanation of each point of the schedule. The hour of class is divided and a teacher knows just what she has to do each of the sixty minutes. She is also given a catechism and a book containing the instructions she must prepare, a chapter a lesson, in the exact order in which she must give them.

We grade the children entering for the first time according to their grades in school, whether they have made their First Communion or not, whether they have ever studied catechism or not. In any case, they need the fundamentals and these can be given them only according to their mental capacity. After the first and succeeding years, they are promoted, if deserving, regardless of their grade in school.

In general, the courses are so arranged that each year all the fundamentals found in all preceding courses are repeated in richer fashion, new ones are added and also new bible stories. The object is contant repetition of essentials with enough new matter to prevent monotony and a fuller treatment to keep pace in completeness of doctrine with the child's increasing mental power. The lessons furnish the teacher with all the theology she requires and should arouse in her a lively interest which she will pass on to her children.

One of our books has been used in a number of Catholic schools as a text for fourth grade children. It is *Catholic Bible Stories* and is well illustrated. Woven into the stories are the doctrines of sin, four of the sacraments, the church, heaven, hell, purgatory, etc. I am told that the children go ahead by themselves and have it read in a week or so, and that they know it, too. Yet they are not tired of it even at the end of the year. It isn't like studying, it's like reading fairy stories. They learn far more in this way and remember better what they learn than they do with matter they have had to pore over and have explained in class. I once assisted at several classes in English in one of our public high schools. The teacher asked the meaning of the expression "sweet as a bed of violets." At once the violets lost their fragrance.

We teachers of religion have the cream of all subjects to teach, a subject that appeals to every pupil, a subject infinitely rich in material, a subject worth while, a subject that calls for the best that is in us.[29]

There you have her method, explained by herself. Her philosophy of religious education, if you will. In his discourse to youth chaplains, Pope Pius XII himself warned: "Beware of being satisfied with formulas learned by heart." For that matter, a great number of our priests follow the custom of opening their sermons with an anecdote or story to immediately catch and hold the attention of their listeners and then tie it up with the lesson in doctrine or morals they wish to impart. And so to the average reader the opposition

[29] Teaching the Other Half. *Journal of Religious Instruction.* 1:471–476, June 1931.

met by the method of Josephine is surprising, if not confusing.

We are fortunate in having an expert in the field explain that as well as to give us his candid appraisal of her work in general. He is Father Francis Harold Drinkwater, diocesan inspector of schools in England, and editor of *The Sower*, a journal of Catholic education.

Father Drinkwater:

It must have been during the nineteen-twenties that I made the acquaintance of a slim book from America, bound in black cloth, called *To the Heart of the Child*. It was a book for lay-catechists, not for children. It had been published several years before, in 1918, and had a preface by Father John J. Wynne, S.J., who made large claims for the book, which, on looking through its pages I found myself agreeing were not too large.

The books of Reverend Dr. Thomas E. Shields were known to me already. Here was something else from America, something even more practical (it seemed) than the Shields books, good as they were; some one who was evidently a teacher of genius pouring that genius into the teaching of religion, looking at children with a fresh mind and telling them about God in a way that fully justified the rather odd-sounding title of the book. For some years in my little periodical [*The Sower*], I had been arguing that the teaching of the Faith ought to be a matter of interest, joy, and love, and here was some one who was not arguing about it but actually doing it! Naturally, I was immensely taken with her way of teaching doctrine through narrative, with her easy uncatechismic language, with her forthright spur-of-the-moment blackboard sketches.

After all this time, I cannot remember how that first edition of to *The Heart of the Child* came my way. It may have been on sale in London, as the American address of the publishers (Encyclopedia Press, Inc.) is crossed out and an address in Kingsway substituted in my handwriting. But for some reason or other, no further echoes of Josephine Van Dyke Brownson came across the Atlantic, and I never heard of the later developments in Detroit, nor of her death during the war, until the other day. But the book itself has always been one of my most cherished possessions. In one of our early aid-books we adapted two or three of her blackboard sketches (with due acknowledgment in the text, I am glad to find), and they are still in use in more recent books which have replaced it. So altogether I have every reason to be thankful to her, and am glad to have this opportunity of paying a debt of gratitude.

Miss Brownson's work cannot be appreciated without understanding the background from which she was reacting so courageously. In 1918, according to Father Wynne's preface, she had already been catechising in Detroit for twenty years, and the book which aroused my enthusiasm in the twenties had existed in the form of type-written notes at the close of the nineteenth century.

The nineteenth century, as those of us who can remember it can testify, was in Europe the opposite of the golden age of catechetics, and no doubt all the European customs, bad and good, crossed the Atlantic with the immigrant Catholics. There were good teachers then as always, but they were snowed under by bad teaching-traditions. Memory, verbal memory, is still too often an object of exaggerated worship, but in those pre-Pius X days, it seemed to be everything. Dullness and boredom, if not worse, were taken for granted, in church as in catechism class; no pictures, except perhaps a few ugly or frightening ones; no admission for young children to Confession or Communion; no explanation (except of course the meaningless explanations in the catechisms) of what the Mass was all about. Yes, there were teachers and missioners who saw the need of livening things up; but their way of doing so was (far too often) to sprinkle their discourses with horror-stories of awful warnings, which are still extant in the story collections of those times. Even in my own church, about twenty years ago, I remember a holy missioner telling the whole school about two children who went off playing instead of going to Sunday Mass and were struck by lightning from heaven, and all that was left of them were two little heaps of ashes on the road. Stories like that—many of them about what happened to people lacking in reverence to the Blessed Sacrament—were certainly interesting, even thrilling; but dullness would have been better.

It was Josephine Brownson's greatness that she reacted strongly against the educational mistakes of the past, not in any negative fashion, but by showing the more excellent way. Dullness was the enemy, and she was determined to escape from it. From the very beginning she was quite clear that the children—the public school children she was concerned with—were going to love the Faith and enjoy learning about it.

"Unless the class becomes a joy to pupils and to teacher," she said, "it will never be the success it should be. And it will be to us a joy only when we love our children and love to work for them. This mutual love will do more for their eternal salvation than memorizing the entire catechism."

From the very beginning she insisted upon appealing to the eye and the hand as well as the ear: "a blackboard is indispensable," she said, and gave detailed suggestions for what we now call work-books. From the very beginning she evidently stood no nonsense from the catechism fanatics.

"The instructions are so arranged that the catechism may be dispensed with when feasible," she said firmly in that 1918 book, and the same sentence in identical words occurs in every one of her subsequent books. In these later books she printed some catechism answers in italics, as an indication that they should be learned, but when you come to reckon them up, and allow for the repetitions, there seem to be less than twenty such answers through all the grades. For her, the catechism was definitely a teacher's book, not a children's book. "The catechism may be dispensed with when feasible" —that was the basic Declaration of Independence which made genuine joyous teaching *possible* for her and her helpers.

"The catechism," says Mr. F. J. Sheed grimly in a recent book called *Are We Really Teaching Religion?*, "makes it possible for people to teach doctrine without knowing doctrine," which, of course, is not teaching at all. When the catechism *is* used, Miss Brownson always said, it should follow explanation and not precede it. Every one says that now, but not every one sees that the step to the catechism words cannot genuinely be made by children of primary school age, unless the catechism is to be translated into child-language, in which case it would no longer be what we call a catechism. I am not attacking catechisms, any more than Josephine Brownson did; all we say is, let us use them to *help,* and not to ruin everything!

The teaching of the Catholic Faith, Josephine realized, is essentially the telling of a *Story.* A story about a *Person.* About a Person and what He does for *You,* for *Us.* So that book of 1918 goes straight through from Creation to the final Church Triumphant, taking in all the doctrines on the way; even the side-doctrines (the Four Marks of the Church, for instance) are thrown into narrative form when possible.

Then, in the later years, when she gradually produced full aid-books all through the grades, look at the titles she gave them:

Come unto Me
Feed My Lambs
Come and See
Keep My Commandments
Thou art Peter
Living Water
I am the Vine

Each of these titles, you may say, is a vivid picture of Jesus Christ in action; that is what Catholic doctrine *is*, that is the Good News according to Josephine. And surely she was right there!

Not for a moment would I claim that her books, or any one else's books, are the last word in perfection. It seems to me a small imperfection that some of them are trying to be a pupil's book and a teacher's book at the same time: on one page is a picture for the child, on another page the teacher is saying: "Shall we play at so and so?" or "Who will come to the blackboard?" Less trivial are some shortcomings, not the fault of the authoress at all, but the inevitable trailing wisps of various mental fog-patches prevailing in the nineteenth century: such things as some rather materialistic sounding and rather too terrifying-for-children descriptions of hell (and purgatory too!), a too dogmatic certainty about what happens to unbaptized babies, a too "fundamentalist" way with the Old Testament story itself and with the moral difficulties it often presents,—and yet how could she have been more up to date in such things when it is only since her death that Pope Pius XII has put into our hands the key —the key of the varying literary forms employed by the inspired writers—which unlocks most of those scripture problems?

Such imperfections in her books could probably be ironed out, and the points in which she was ahead of her times—is *still* ahead of the times—would only stand out the more clearly. One such point is the all-important one of *language*.

After the teacher's own union with God, by overflowing charity, (which necessarily counts most, since religion is "caught rather than taught"), the most important thing in teaching religion is language. Not merely the vocabulary used, but the whole way of combining words to get a desired effect—or express a given meaning, if you like—on the minds and imaginations of such and such hearers. In the beginning was the Word. When God speaks to men—at any rate to men collectively—He has to make use of words. The Church too is constantly struggling to find words that will keep intact *and* transmit accurately the truths entrusted to her. In the end, it is the individual priest or catechist who has to find the right words for each new learner of the Faith. Most of us priests do this badly with children at first, because no one has ever showed us how, and because our minds are full of the wrong kind of words for the purpose; and as most teachers and catechists take their cue from priests or from books written by priests, the prospects of the children are rather gloomy.

In this matter of language, Josephine certainly came to the rescue. Open any of her books at any page, and you will find the simple language of everyday talk, energetic and purposeful and entirely intelligible. In narrative it will be rapid and vivid and visual, in doctrinal explanation it will be clear, effective and very rarely other than theologically accurate. Indeed, sometimes she improves on our regular expressions: where we say "There are three Persons in God" she prefers to say "God is in three Persons," which will strike many as being better. When she says anything, it really is communication. To illustrate this point, here is an incident she tells us herself in her booklet *Stopping the Leak*.

"In giving an instruction to teachers on the Fall of the Angels, I used a word which I thought peculiarly fitting and expressive. Of course I did not tell the teachers this. One day a teacher showed me a little composition written by one of her pupils and said: "I gave my class the instruction on the Angels. One little girl was so interested that the next week she presented me with an envelope. On opening it, I found that she had gone home and written the instruction. Here it is." I read the little composition and there was the very word, at third hand, which I had selected so carefully."

In other ways, too, she is so practical: all the suggestions, for instance, reiterated a hundred times, on every detail of how the lessons should be conducted. The insistence on keeping to the schedule or time-table of each session—for school purposes one would have to call it too rigid, just as her verbatim lesson-material would be called spoon-feeding the teacher, but she is justified by the fact which she never forgets: that she is dealing largely with amateur teachers and with children who know little or nothing of their religion and have little time to learn it in.

First impressions, too—she understands how important it is that they should be "full and rich, for first impressions endure:" another reason for keeping back the catechism until its ground has been covered in other ways, because whatever the catechism may be, it is not "full and rich." Her review-questioning, too, is always practical, and one notices that she improves the questions with experience. For instance, in the 1918 book she asks: "What do you mean by

the Immaculate Conception?" In the 1934 edition this becomes: "What do you call the fact that Mary started life
without original sin?" Which is easier for the children and
just as effective for the immediate purpose.

The complete concentric series of her books, repeating
the basic doctrine eight times over to give it fresh and whole
to each age-group, so that a child of any age can be put into
a religious class of its own grade without missing anything
essential, surely deserves to be called a triumph of intellectual organizing. All the scripture history is got into the series
also, but if some or even most of it is missed by some child
it can't be helped; all the absolute essentials of belief and
practice will still be encountered. How far the total scheme
works out in actual practice, only those who have operated
it can decide. I still confess to a lingering backward glance
at that 1918 book with its spare and workmanlike simplicity.
If she had been writing the later books today, she would
have treated the Old Testament episodes with a far more
Messianic, "typical," and liturgical outlook. But it certainly
is an interesting occupation to follow some thread of doctrine
—say, our Lord's Resurrection, or the Church—through all
the eight volumes and see how she changes or develops the
treatment in each. How wonderfully fresh she keeps through
it all, is the reflection occasioned by such a bit of research.
After the third grade, there is not so much gradual deepen-
ing of the ideas and treatment as one might expect, but I feel
sure she knows what she is doing is driving home the sheer
essentials.

Something special must be said about the Readers for
the first two grades, *Come to Me* and *Feed My Lambs*. These
are genuine *pupils'* books, to supplement the instruction of
the teacher. Without claiming much competence as a judge
of books for such small children, I feel sure that the writing

in these two books has the right directness and warmth that is needed. ("No catechism is required," says Josephine in the preface to these). The little verses especially strike the right note:

In my airplane high I fly
Till I almost touch the sky.

But no matter where I go
Up above the clouds or low,

God is there in every place.
How I'd love to see His face!

Now that goes one better than the bald statement that "God is everywhere" (though she puts that in too afterwards).

Or this, after Holy Communion:

I hold my darling Jesus,
I will not let Him go,
He's come clear down from heaven
Because He loves me so.

We have two or three writers in England too who are good at this kind of doctrine-in-verse-or hymns, but it looks as if Josephine got there first.

She had, of course, one great advantage over the school teacher; her children came to her of their own free will. This meant that she had to interest them to keep them; but it also meant that the teacher-pupil relationship was likely to be good, was at any rate not poisoned at the source with unwillingness and compulsion and punishment. Hers was a school where the only rule was love, and if the pupils had ever felt that the supply of love had run out, there was noth-

ing to stop them from leaving. This free and natural relationship explains (for instance) why she can say to her teachers:
"Never omit questioning the class regarding attendance at
Sunday Mass;" a procedure which most of us would discour-
age in schools. Even Josephine mentions safeguards, and
says: "Do not hold up any child for the disapproval of the
others." But the fact is, if the teacher-pupil relationship, or
rather, the teacher-and-class relationship, is right, all kinds
of things become possible that one dare not ask for in schools
generally. Compulsory education may be necessary, but a
price is paid for it.

In the end, I come back to that marvellous little twenty-
page booklet she wrote in 1925: *Stopping the Leak*. Booklet
is the wrong word—manifesto, it should be called. If the
successors of St. Peter ever decide to declare women Doctors
of the Church, the name of Josephine Brownson, on the
strength of this little book, should have its place in the queue
after great names like Catherine of Siena and Teresa of
Avila. It is a great little book, bursting with the essence of
the apostolate. I would put its short, stirring sentences in the
same class as Napoleon's eve-of-battle proclamations to his
soldiers or (to take a holier instance) that first meditation in
the *Spiritual Exercises* of St. Ignatius. Its opening words are
like a trumpet call:

"Hundreds of thousands of our Catholic children are
being lost to the Church through inadequate religious instruction. Such is the case throughout the length and breadth
of our country, in the large city, in the small town, on the
isolated farm . . . In a few years, priests will be devoting
their lives and exerting every ounce of their strength to bring
into the Church by missions and convert classes a few of the
many that are ours now for the asking. Oh, let us shake off
this torpor and stretch out a hand to save the souls of thou-

sands of little children that are hourly perishing at our door. You do not see them? Have you ever looked? Walk along any street and question any group of children you meet. You will find among them children who have been robbed of their birthright, children who have been told nothing of the inheritance that is theirs, children who at a word from us will attend a Catholic school, children who will gladly come to our instructions, children whose parents we can bring back to the household of the Faith, children whose young lives death will claim and who will die without having received a Sacrament."

Trumpet-call, isn't it? We call that spirit "kerygmatic" nowadays, a word that I feel Josephine Brownson never heard of, but she shared the thing all right, the pentecostal breath itself.

The other side of Napoleon's genius comes to mind as we read on through the other pages of the pamphlet: his infinite capacity for taking pains in the detailed staff-work that forgets nothing, provides for every possible contingency, and compels success. Everything she has to say about preparing lessons, about conduct in class, about encouraging attendance and Mass-going, about the teaching of prayers, about review questions, singing, and so on,—it is right on the bull's-eye, and every practical question is alive with the urgency and understanding of the apostle; it's just like Paul in his epistles. Yes, she is writing largely for untrained amateur helpers, but one can't help wishing that every Catholic teacher in the world, from the highest university downwards, could read these burning twenty-two pages. They would all get *some* new idea from them, or at least catch some spark of the experienced enthusiasm that blazes through every word.

There is a saying of holy Scripture that she was fond of using to encourage her recruits and we will end with it here because it is surely as true of Josephine herself as of any worker in God's wide vineyard: "They that instruct many to justice shall shine as the stars for all eternity." Or if you prefer Monsignor Knox (another advantage she lacked and would have loved): "Starry-bright for ever their glory, who have taught many the right way." There must be many families now in Detroit, and many perhaps elsewhere too, who are going the right way under God's grace because of Josephine Van Dyke Brownson.

Father Drinkwater's estimate (sent in a letter to Josephine's sister Elizabeth, Christmas, 1953) has been given verbatim and in full because of his earned reputation as the greatest living authority in the field of religious instruction and especially because every single sentence in it is significant. Incidentally, its date is important too: he wrote it nearly thirty years after his first acquaintance with her works: it certainly may be said to represent his considered judgement.

And in deference to his judgement as well as an additional courtesy to our readers, we are including as an Appendix to this volume the complete text of Josephine's *Stopping the Leak.*

A note on her follow-through technique and practice should complete this chapter on her method.

One of her strongest points was her belief in the *importance* of the work of bringing children to know and love God. And she insisted that the children should be made to feel that nothing was so important in the lives of their C.I.L. teachers as their religion classes. But this was not to be done at the expense of interest. "Our classes will not remain small because children refuse to come, but because we fail to interest those who do come."

It has been mentioned that she also insisted on all her teachers adhering faithfully to the C.I.L. schedule. Here is that schedule:

Taking attendance	5 minutes
Recitation and assignment of lesson	15 minutes
Questions on weekly practice	5 minutes
Teaching prayers	10 minutes
Instruction	20 minutes
Hymn	5 minutes

It is self-explanatory, except perhaps for the weekly practice. That was a definite thing the children must do in connection with the last lesson. The children readily entered in to the spirit of the practice because it was always checked.

Of paramount importance, however, was the instruction. Full time was to be given to it (the subject known thoroughly, the presentation rehearsed, even the manner studied in every detail), and nothing must be allowed to interrupt it.

Besides the schedule, there were general monthly meetings of the teachers that followed up every phase of the work, such as lessons, attendance, parent co-operation, distribution of notes with questions and information, the needs of the coming month, and anything exceptional. These meetings—always held on the same day of the month—were opened by a priest, very often by Father Frederick T. Hoeger, C.S.Sp., or Father Louis Weitzman, S.J., who then gave the group a solid spiritual conference.

The annual meeting at the close of the school year was on a broader scale and included exhibits of the children's activities from all the Centers of the diocese.

The final eighth grade examinations were held at the University of Detroit; there the graduation ceremonies were also held. The location was an incentive. "The grander we make it all," said Josephine, "the more desirable graduation is in the eyes of the children." Always that Napoleonic attention to detail.

The June breakfast (Dutch-treat, for this was an apostolate of the poor) was attended by the directors of all the Centers. It concluded the year's labors.

CHAPTER SIX

"In the Beginning was the Word"

IF, IN HER PRESENCE, SOME ONE HAD REFERRED TO JOSE-phine as a writer, she would have answered that her books were written primarily as texts to be followed by the C.I.L. and any other catechist or group of them who believed in her method of religious instruction. That, of course, is true. But it is equally true that if she had not organized the C.I.L., but had only written her books, they alone would have stamped her life as one of achievement, and would have made her reputation secure.

They were, naturally, the official C.I.L. texts throughout all of its nearly thirty-five years; they were also, as we shall note more specifically later, used as the texts of a number of other religious instruction organizations. But aside from their classroom use, they had a wide general circulation.[30] So much so that it might justly be called another apostolate.

They were also read and used by countless families who did not have an opportunity to get formal instructions. Mothers, especially young mothers, who aspired to be in-struments in opening the minds of their children to the things of God sent her letters of gratitude. Josephine herself admitted that the call for her books came "not only from cities, but also from mothers living out in the country, where they have not teachers and must themselves teach their little

[30] For example, by 1948, her *Learn of Me*, in its paper bound edition alone, had a circulation of nearly 60,000 copies.

ones, or let them go without the most important of all knowledge—religious instruction."

Very many of these families had themselves received little or no religious instruction, and they therefore would have found the question and answer catechism of little help if, as was unlikely, they had tried to use it at all. Her books, combining Old and New Testament stories as well as the fundamentals of doctrinal and moral teaching, all presented in attractive narrative form, were the perfect answer to their problem.

Her first published work was entitled *Stopping the Leak*. Its circulation was wide; its effect startling; for few people realized even the enormity of the problem.

What theologians call the salvific will of Christ simply means that He desires that every one will get to heaven, and implements that desire by giving them the means. This wish of Christ is not confined to any race or social or economic class; it is meant for all. Therefore His religion is meant for all; and hence one who has a true understanding and appreciation of it will never give it up. They would rather die than do so. But the fact is that every year nearly a half million American Catholics do give up the practice of their religion.[31] Why? Obviously because they do not know and love it, at least not enough to keep it. In fine, they have not been instructed in their religion, or the instruction they received has not proved effective.[32]

[31] In 1952, a professional research firm employed by the Catholic Digest reported that in the twenty years before the study 1,434,000 nominal Catholics became Protestants and 2,529,000 nominal Catholics discontinued the practice of any religion. Report printed in the *Catholic Digest,* June and July, 1952.

[32] "We know that there is a large leakage in the Catholic Church. How large it is no one knows. The causes of the leakage are fairly well known: lack of religious schooling, indifference to religious practice in nominally Catholic families (often as a result of mixed marriages), absorp-

This loss to the Church in our own country alone of nearly a thousand souls a day is usually referred to as leakage. Josephine so referred to it in her first book.[33] Today not only the fact but a reasonably accurate estimate of its extent is well known; frequent articles are written on the subject. But Josephine recognized the extent and the havoc of this leakage fifty years ago. In fact, she devoted her life to stemming it.

The remainder of her foreword to *Stopping the Leak* is a plea to the average lay Catholic to share in her work, and the body of the booklet instructs such a one in the technique of imparting religious instruction systematically and fruitfully.

Following this booklet, she wrote the "Learn of Me" series of eight textbooks to which we have already referred. Each volume or course includes doctrine, morals and nearly all the stories of the Old and New Testaments. The eight courses are like a set of eight Chinese eggs in which the tiniest egg—complete in itself—is enclosed in a larger egg, and that in turn in a still larger one, and so on. Each successive course repeats in fuller fashion the principal doctrines taught in all the previous courses and adds new material. Like the eighth, the eighth grade course is the most comprehensive and covers all the fundamental doctrines taught in the seven preceding grades. For example, the Incarnation is

---

tion in an atmosphere (whether in school or out of school) hostile to Catholicism, alienation from Catholicism through marriages with non-Catholics or divorce and re-marriage, alienation through the practice of birth control, or simple neglect of religious practice through laziness"—Thomas J. Burke, S.J., *America* 91:37–39 April 10, 1954. It still boils down to either no religious instruction or ineffective religious instruction.

[33] In an article, Loss from Leakage, Josephine is quoted: "All America would soon be Catholic if the terrible leakage in the Church could be stopped." John J. O'Connor, *Ave Maria.* 40:619–622, Nov. 17, 1934.

taught eight times, each time more fully. Thus there is constant repetition without monotony.

It required a strong will as well as a mastery of the subject to carry out such a plan; also a keen knowledge of the intelligence level of each group. The gradation of each book: the groundwork always the same, the superstructure always differing, constituted a task that was far more difficult than the writing of eight books for any one age level.

But the accomplishment achieved results which still have not been obtained by any other method. For example, any pupil who knew the matter in the book for his grade knew enough to make his First Communion at his age. There was also the advantage of being able to place the pupil, upon entrance, in the same grade in which he was in his other studies; for each course is adapted to the mentality of pupils of that grade and does not depend upon knowledge previously acquired. Hence, for example, a fifteen year old boy who had received no previous religious instruction, could be put into the class of his own age level, and not in a class of six year olds where his presence would embarrass him and confuse them. Still another advantage of her method was that, due to the fullness of the text, the child did not suffer as much through poor preparation or poor background on the part of the teacher, whether the teacher be a parent or one of Josephine's own staff.

But in this vale of tears, nothing is all sweetness and light. And Josephine had to pay the penalties of leadership. Any biography of her which sought to evade recording them would be unworthy of her own integrity.

"Religion," she held, "is not a progressive subject like mathematics. A mathematics pupil learns simple addition and subtraction, later fractions, still later equations. Religion is an integral subject. Each year a child should get a complete course."

Although she proved in action the truth of her dictum, many teachers of religion did not agree with her, and exercised their right of saying so. An honest and frank difference of opinion, and so all to the good. But not so the criticism that she disparaged the catechism; a charge which Father Drinkwater has more than adequately disproved for us, and we hope for you.

But the real obstacles were less tangible than these; they were more an antagonistic sentiment than a judgement.

Rome, in popular thought ponderously deliberate and slow, is really the vanguard as well as the final authority of the Church. For example, the social reforms of Pope Leo XIII in 1891 had to await our own day for practical application. Also the problem of racial relations; and so on. The Church's traditional teaching of woman as man's spiritual equal is based on the example of Christ. But if equal spiritually, then she is necessarily equal in the perception of spiritual truth through which salvation is obtained. Despite the official position of the Church and the actual exemplification in the theological acumen of such minds as Teresa of Avila (a mystical theologian), Therese of Lisieux (an ascetical theologian), Catherine of Siena, and a host of others, yet a woman writing in the field of theology is still suspect. Conceded good intentions, her capability is denied. Naturally Josephine got her share of that.

In a letter to Father Aloysius J. Heeg, S.J., dated November 24, 1930, she remarked: "One of the Jesuits suggested my signing my name J. Van Dyke Brownson. If some one would only hand me a D.D. I'd be all set!" [34]

[34] After she received the honorary LL.D. she was often referred to as Dr. Brownson. Cf. O'Connor. *op. cit.*

To mitigate the effectiveness of the implication, several of the leading Catholic publishers made suggestions to her. For example, Francis A. Fink, managing editor of Our Sunday Visitor Press, recommended naming Father Leo De Barry as a collaborator. Since her writings had frequently benefited by his theological counsel, the suggestion was followed and the title pages of the Our Sunday Visitor edition of her works read: "In collaboration with Rev. Leo De Barry, S.T.D., archdiocesan director of the Society for the Propagation of the Faith, Detroit."

Likewise, on the receipt of one of her manuscripts, Frank Bruce, late president of the Bruce Publishing Company, informed her that she "must secure the names of two priests as co-authors."

Father Drinkwater has shown that some criticism of her usage of Sacred Scripture is based on knowledge not yet available in her day. To demand foreknowledge of her is one thing; that she was denied access to contemporary knowledge is quite another. To keep abreast in the Scriptural sciences she sought membership in the Catholic Biblical Association, but, at least at that time (1937–1938) the laity was not admitted, and she was refused. She sought the intervention of some of her priest friends, but they could give her only the crumbs of consolation.

Another belittling innuendo aimed at her writings was that they were deficient in modern psychology. Ironical that, for in nothing did her greatness shine more brightly. She began giving religious instruction when she was a child, and as a child she was taken with the wonder of it all. The eternal love of God for His children and the adventure that was hers in helping to make that love mutual. To bring the two lovers together! It was her genius that she never lost that sense of holy wonder, that sense of holy love. Never lost it herself, and was able to impart it to so many of her teachers, to so many of her pupils. Her knowledge of child psychology was so true that it had no defects that needed to be hidden with a cloak of technical jargon. But this is a professional matter, —child psychology; so let us again enter the testimony of an expert.

A priest writing in the *Ecclesiastical Review:*

"You want to win the heart of the child first for God and then for its own best interests, which entail the best interests likewise of its fellow children. But what is the surest and quickest way into the citadel which is guarded from within by passion and selfishness? Is it through the head and the intellectual memory? Or is through feeling or emotion? Neither. It is through the imagination, which, if rightly directed, spontaneously acts on the one side upon the feelings and on the other side upon the intelligence and memory. This is good pedagogy, *because it is true psychology,* while it is sanctioned by the practice of Christ, the greatest of Masters, and by that of all the teachers who in the course of time have won the hearts of children.

"It goes without saying that women, intelligent women, women whose native instincts have not been smothered by blankets of artificial pedagogy, spontaneously adopt this method. The method, however natural though it be and spontaneous, requires intelligent adjustment and application, such as it receives in this admirable little volume, *To the Heart of the Child,* by Josephine Brownson." [35]

Besides the manuscripts of some of her lecture courses, there were left unpublished at her death two others: one of three hundred and fifty pages on the Old Testament; the other, one of one hundred and twenty three pages on Evolution. The former seems never to have been submitted for

[35] *American Ecclesiastical Review.* 59:642–643, Dec. 1918.

publication; the latter had. Regarding it, a leading Catholic publisher had made these recommendations: an attitude of greater impartiality toward the sincere proponents of evolution; philosophic rather than scriptural proofs in metaphysical argument; the ontological argument in proof of the creation of the soul of man, rather than the teaching authority of the Church; and a glossary informally defining the technical terms used. But she never found the time to make the requested revision.

So much for Josephine's writings. Let us now go on to some of her other activities.

CHAPTER SEVEN

"So that nothing may be lost"

THE SUCCESS OF THE CATHOLIC INSTRUCTION LEAGUE stamped Josephine as an authority among teachers of religion throughout the English-speaking world. This resulted in her counsel being sought not only through voluminous correspondence but by numerous invitations to give lectures and even courses. Naturally the C.I.L. had first call on her time, and so she could accept comparatively few such requests. But as part of the record of the general acknowledgment of her leadership, at least some of those accepted should be mentioned.

Following her lecture at St. John's College, Toledo, Ohio, in March of 1927, Father William A. Ryan, S.J., wrote her: "I admit I have been aided in my catechetical work, but likewise in my teaching of other branches."

More than a decade after her lecture on the work of the C.I.L. delivered before the First Provincial Catechetical Congress of the Confraternity of Christian Doctrine, at La Crosse, Wisconsin, in April of 1939, Sister M. Cherubim, S.S.N.D., wrote her in deep appreciation of it.

In the summer of 1930, Josephine went to Las Vegas, New Mexico, at the invitation of Father John J. Sigstein to give a course on "Teaching Religion" to a group of forty members of his Society of Missionary Catechists from centers in New Mexico, California, and Texas. "Miss Brownson used as a basis for her course, which lasted about two weeks, her booklet, *Stopping the Leak*, supplementing it with her own interesting experiences in teaching religion to public school children. At the end of each day's session our Sisters ("Catechists" in those days) were given an opportunity to seek her advice in their own problems concerning the teaching of these children. I shall never forget Miss Brownson's remarkable story-telling ability when she demonstrated her method of teaching. I can still see her impersonating the aggressive Goliath in her story of David and the shepherd boy." Just how vivid her courses were may be inferred from the fact that this report by one of her audience, Sister Blanche Marie, O.L.V.M. (then Catechist Richardson), was written twenty-four years later!

Under Father Sigstein's devoted direction, this Society became the Our Lady of Victory Missionary Sisters, with Motherhouse and Novitiate at Victory Noll, Huntington, Indiana.[36] In 1931, their Superior invited Josephine to give them two Christian doctrine teaching courses. Her typed manuscript of the forty lessons is still extant, but was never published.

In October of 1936, before the National Council of Catholic Women session of Catholic Action Week in Dubuque, Iowa, she delivered an address on "The Confraternity of Christian Doctrine in the Home." Her keynote was: "Educational work with children will often fail if the background of the whole family is not changed." *The Witness*, the official organ of the archdiocese of Dubuque, thought so highly of her lecture that they printed it in full in their issue of October 29, 1936.

Josephine was invited to conduct three classes for teach-

[36] By 1947, this community numbered 280 Sisters, attended 338 missions, and had 46,474 children under instruction.

ers at the Confraternity of Christian Doctrine Conference in Hartford, Connecticut, in October, 1938; and at its Cincinnati Conference in 1939, she was requested to give three talks on three consecutive days.

In that same year of 1939, she made two Ohio appearances: in May she delivered the Commencement Address of the Mercy School of Nursing graduation exercises, held in the Ursuline Auditorium, Toledo; and later in the year, addressed the Catholic Collegiate Association at their annual breakfast at the University Club, Cleveland.

When Father John F. O'Hara, C.S.C., then president of the University of Notre Dame, was asked to conduct the American Social Service Mission to Venezuela in 1939, he wrote Josephine: "I should like very much to have you as a member of the Commission. There are many problems in regard to religious education in the public schools of Venezuela to be solved, and your advice would be invaluable."

Of course, she accepted. The party sailed from New York to Caracas. Following the reception and dinner in the home of President and Signora Contreras, there were sightseeing tours and then a series of lectures. She spoke on a child's need of religious instruction to enable him to become a good citizen here as well as hereafter, and how the Catholic Instruction League was laboring to meet that need in the diocese of Detroit.

Of course, she was also often called upon to give impromptu talks. Any school or institution she visited hailed the opportunity of hearing her, knowing that they would be given something worthwhile. Even on her holidays. For example, from Goderich she wrote of acceding to Mother Gertrude's request to give a talk to the Ursulines at Brescia Hall in London, Ontario.

Regarding her speaking engagements, this paragraph from one of her letters is quite to the point:

"I know you will think I have grown quite mercenary not to have accepted your cordial invitation to speak. But I would be gallivanting all over the country if I didn't set a price. Then, too, it would scarcely be fair to those who are paying me for a talk. I can't stand the constant travel, pulling up stakes, returning so tired I can't work for a day, and in the meantime the work has piled up and must be done. Of course, I would go to any pains, free, to really start Centers. But when people look to be entertained at a banquet, I ask a fee. I never used to, but I have been asked around too much."

Our postscript: the letter was written in 1940, when she was sixty years of age. Of course, she was never paid for speaking at congresses, conferences, conventions, etc.; in fact, she had to defray the expenses of her round trips; but this was usually taken care of by the C.I.L.

Her lectures were extra-curricular activities only in the sense of being exercised outside her home territory. Josephine was not one to dilute her energies or her interests. In fact, few people go through life with her singleness of purpose. Wherever she went and whom ever she met were viewed as grist for her mill: either prospective children to teach or potential teachers of her children. As a result of her being so engrossed in the C.I.L., she took no part and, truth to tell, very little interest in other movements or activities. Would her own work have had so wide a scope, would it have been so well organized, so efficient and so effective had she been otherwise? If she had a one-track mind, the track led to a planned place and carried a specific cargo; and it arrived with it.

"The freshness, vividness and attractiveness" [37] of her

[37] Amer. Eccles. Review. *op. cit.*

texts and method made them widely adopted. Some indication of this extension of her influence should surely be made here.

"I found your dear note on my return home. You're a brick, and that says everything! . . . I wish you would start a C.I.L. in Grand Rapids," Josephine wrote Mary Kay Kirby, on September 15, 1934. Later in the year, Miss Kirby, who knew of Josephine's work when she lived in Detroit, told a meeting of the League of Catholic Women of Grand Rapids (Michigan) about it and offered to help organize a C.I.L. there. The offer was enthusiastically accepted. Through a steady stream of letters, Josephine is constantly at her side, counselling, encouraging. December 10, 1934: "I got your most interesting letter and congratulate you on the great things you have accomplished." February 25, 1935: "Don't get discouraged. Unless the Lord build a house, they labor in vain who seek to build it. Take it easy; you can only do what you can, and you have made a fine beginning. We have been many years at it, and besides people in a small town have much less daring than those in a big city.[38] If some priest would interest a fine teacher, she might induce others. Teachers here were a bit wary at first, too. Look for hardworking, poor girls. Club members are no good." April 11, 1935: "Congratulations on your *two* Centers!" May 9, 1935: "Our breakfast will be at the Detroit-Leland, after 8:30 Mass in St. Aloysius Church, Sunday, May 26. We would love to welcome you and your teachers. . . . Congratulations on your success." By 1950, the Grand Rapids C.I.L. had 54 teachers instructing 824 children; while during the year they

[38] Surely Josephine was using the affectionate dimunitive here! Grand Rapids, the second largest city in the state, has a population in excess of 176,000.

had prepared 15 for Baptism, 220 for First Communion, and 177 for Confirmation.[39]

On March 3, 1932, Father J. J. Silva, chaplain of the nun's academy in Montevideo, wrote Josephine: "At the time of the distribution of prizes, I made a little speech about your magnificent method, and I promised the girls I would write you in order to let you know the wonderful results of the first trial of your method of teaching catechism in Uruguay, and probably in South America."

On the recommendation of Gabrielle Bouscaren, Josephine's books were used by the Department of Religious Instruction of the Cincinnati chapter of the International Federation of Catholic Alumnae in their fourteen Centers, the chairman of the department, Eileen McBreen, reported in August of 1940. "Josephine was really the godmother of our organization, as it was through her advice that we began these week-day instructions, the only system that gets any results; and she also taught us how to teach and to run a Center," wrote Miss Bouscaren on March 21, 1943. She had been introduced to Josephine's method and texts some twenty years before by her brother, Father T. Lincoln Bouscaren, S.J.

On January 3, 1936, Sister M. Aurelia, O.S.F., joint author with Father Felix M. Kirsch, O.F.M. Cap., of the three volume *Practical Aids for Catholic Teachers,* thanked Josephine for permission to use her material in the Pittsburgh Diocesan Normal School religion class for nuns.

Sister M. Veronica Bentz, O.S.B., wrote Josephine: "In a recent letter from Rev. Aloysius J. Heeg, S.J., he assures me that most of his inspiration for his work came from your writings."

[39] L. G. Miller, God before Breakfast. *Liguorian.* Sept. 1950.

But surely one of her crowning glories was summed up by Archbishop Mooney when he declared that he looked upon the Catholic Instruction League as his Marines. As that famous fighting corps would effect a beach landing and there establish a foothold upon which the Army could have a secure base from which to carry on the operation of complete conquest, so the C.I.L. entered hostile territory, diligently searched out the should-be children of the Church, began an Instruction Center for them and, when it had sufficient enrollment and stability, turned it over to the teaching nuns, and then moved on to another beach head. From these Centers developed Catholic communities, each the nucleus of a parish. Indeed, the 1954 report of the Confraternity specifically states that in sixteen years fourteen parishes had been established in areas initially served in a number of instances by these Instruction Centers.[40]

[40] *The Michigan Catholic.* April 8, 1954.

CHAPTER EIGHT

"None has merited my fear, And none has quite escaped my smile"

A DOMINICAN MISSIONARY AND ASCETICAL WRITER, Father Vincent F. Kienberger, O.P., came to know Josephine well when he was stationed at St. Dominic's in Detroit. He recalls that she not only established a Center there but that "the debt-burdened pastor was heartened by the interest and kindly assistance of Miss Brownson, who helped to lighten the great debt contracted for the school during the grim days of the depression." He also writes that "She scattered the stardust of merriment with a prodigal hand. Her infectious laughter drew around her those who excelled in witticisms and repartees."

And although money and merriment are usually coupled in a different context, any analysis of Josephine's personality and character must take them into consideration, albeit separately.

She had a sense of humor. But how does one go about capturing its memory? The wisp of her smile, the eider down of her laughter,—how bring them back, much less describe them? Does it help to quote her letter to an old friend: "You have been so very silent that I am afraid you are angry or ill. I hope it's only the former."

Or an anecdote. At the wake of a friend whose family

excused their absence on the score of being "unavoidably detained," she glanced at the casket and murmured: "He wouldn't be here either if he were not 'unavoidably detained.'"

But money. That is of this earth, earthly; and as tangible.

An evidence of her detachment from it is the fact that she not only wrote her books but published many of them! Yes, she contracted and paid for their printing and binding, read the proofs, drew and had plates made for the illustrations, publicized them, stocked them in the basement of her home (which occasionally flooded!), shipped them, kept her own accounts, etc. A one person publishing company! Her primary reason for taking on all this additional labor was, of course, to control the prices of her books. Practically all the C.I.L. pupils came from low income families. They had not much to spend over and above necessities and, to them, books, especially religious instruction books, were no necessity. But by keeping their prices at about cost, Josephine was able to achieve a good distribution to them. Total figures are not available, but one book manufacturer's invoice covers a 3,000 copy paper bound edition of *Thou art Peter*. The total cost was $1,015.47, or about thirty four cents a copy. She resold them for fifty cents each, less discounts. Add to that the cost of shipping materials, printing of invoices and statements, review and defective copies, bad debts, etc., and one will see the wisdom in the warning given her in a letter by Father William J. Doran, S.J. "Your selling the books for fifty cents won't enable you to come out even, much less give you a profit. True, it is right to get the price down as low as possible, but you have to live, and you certainly deserve to get something for your labors."

Yes, she was careful with money. Very careful, indeed, when it came to stretching the income of others, especially the poor. But when it came to her own money, there is quite a different story to tell. For example, the C.I.L. teachers planned to raise a purse for her when she was awarded the Laetare Medal. As soon as she got wind of it, she asked them not to; and, of course, that ended the matter. At the same time she received gifts of money from individuals. These she returned with a note which concluded: "So please do not feel hurt at my returning the check; but the thought and the good wishes I am not returning but cherishing."

Reluctant to receive; eager to give: that was Josephine. She encouraged parents to send their children to parish schools, and when the excuse was expense she defrayed it; likewise in fostering vocations to the priesthood, she often helped financially. Obviously, names can not be mentioned in this connection. But surely many gratefully remember. And there are a few records. Here is one for the school year of 1924–1925. Five tuitions paid for boys she sent to the University of Detroit (Jesuit) High School, then on Jefferson avenue. The total is $600.00. The receipts are made out to Josephine Brownson and signed by Rev. R. H. Daly, S.J., principal. What percentage of her salary as a public school teacher did that one sharing of it take? But one should not embarrass even her memory by disclosing her charity. Though it demands mention in any estimate of her character.

In this connection, another pertinent sidelight emerges. She was sometimes referred to as plainly dressed; the word mannish was even used. But one who has shared her wages with others—others, incidentally, who were not relatives or, strictly speaking, even friends—such a one can hardly flourish jewels and gowns and furs. Josephine dressed sensibly with, if you insist, an absence of charm. However, she always dressed like a lady. And of many women who squander fortunes on their apparel as much may not be said.

While on the subject of money, we might mention that up to 1934 all the Catholic Instruction League expenses were defrayed by Josephine and her staff, supplemented by an occasional assist from an organization (the Society of St. Vincent de Paul must be mentioned in particular here) or from an individual (and here the late Theodore F. Mac-Manus must be mentioned in particular). But at one of the C.I.L. meetings in 1934, their devoted friend Father Leo De Barry told them that their work deserved an Auxiliary. The suggestion sprang from his heart, for calculation would have warned him that he risked reprimand in not submitting the idea to the bishop first. But instead, he was given the office of organizing and directing the Catholic Instruction League Auxiliary. Considering that it was in the depth of the depression that this fund raising campaign was begun, the record is very good: $1,085 in 1934; $1,930 in 1935; $1,726 in 1936. Under Archbishop Mooney in 1937 it continued to be officially endorsed. His signed and circulated statement read: "I earnestly hope that the worthy appeal of the Catholic Instruction League Auxiliary will meet with wide and generous support."

Besides financial and moral assistance, the Society of St. Vincent de Paul co-operated in essential phases of the actual labor, such as investigating children's background, as well as spiritualizing it when necessary and possible. To let them know how much she appreciated their help, Josephine often sent the Society a copy of the C.I.L. reports.

But appreciation was one of her strong characteristics. While she believed firmly in her own catechetical method, she was never indifferent to or critical of the work of others in the field. She not only respected it, but from her crowded day took the time and effort to express her admiration and encouragement. We have such letters written to the Right Rev. Monsignor Leon A. McNeill for his Mystical Body of Christ series of religion textbooks; to Sister Mary Rosalia, M.H.S.H., for her Confraternity School Year religion course; and to Father Aloysius J. Heeg, S.J., for his *Practical Helps for the Religion Teacher,* and his *Jesus and I* ("Its simplicity and gentle spirit are just the thing for children," she wrote him).

Naturally, her deepest appreciation was to her own staff. Its members for the most part she personally recruited from her fellow public school teachers. Why? Because they were nearest at hand? Hardly. Of what advantage would their being conveniently available have been to her if they were not suitable for the work? But they were professionally trained and experienced teachers. Yes, and because she appreciated precisely all that that meant she chose them. For she, of course, knew them as they were, and not as the raw-boned, flat-breasted, unimaginative martinets the comic strips (and some parents) pictured them. She knew their flexibility and their enthusiasm. She knew the fine qualities of mind and heart which enabled them day after day to teach, train, coax and persuade thousands of reluctant pupils.[41]

The Catholic Instruction League taught for the most part voluntary pupils. And to keep them coming it had to inspire and retain their interest in the spiritual,—a subject

[41] As Msgr. J. A. Gorham, editor of *The Catholic Educational Review,* has written, it is unfortunate that these fine teachers have as their spokesman "the deceptive, self-righteous and intolerant old peddlers of divisiveness and First Amendment sophistry who are chosen to rasp their dissonant theme year after year at conventions of public school personnel"—*Cath. Educ. Review.* 52:213, March 1954.

for which, all too often, their home life aroused little or no response. And so, from the start, Josephine chose public school teachers to work with. And she never had reason to regret or to change her choice.

"Speaking of her staff she said: "It should be clearly understood that these teachers are not catechists. They are real teachers who instruct children in a course of religion, and they use many of the modern aids of the classroom. They need blackboards, graded textbooks, maps, symbols, and collateral reading materials. They maintain the discipline of the regular courses which is essential to learning."

Josephine recruited literally hundreds of these professional teachers. The majority of them certainly must have felt that whatever pedagogical obligation they owed to their community they had paid in full by the close of their public school classroom day. Yet she was able to persuade them to voluntary overtime; not one or two, but hundreds of them; and not for a day or a week, but many of them year after year. Coupled with the strong persuasion of the cause, there had to have been the personal magnetism of Josephine. And despite her constant insistence (irksome sometimes perhaps, but necessary insistence) on their following her rigid schedule, to say nothing of punctuality, reports, meetings, etc., she won their loyalty and even their affection. The secret was herself. She was their inspiration and their guide. She was their model. The purity of her apostolate called them; her zeal inspired them; her tireless labors challenged them. The last of the old guard, after her death, sent Elizabeth a spiritual bouquet "In memory of our beloved leader, with the loving wishes of the teachers and children of the Catholic Instruction League, Feast of the Nativity, 1942." The depth of their devotion is indicated by the extent of their remembrance: "1,179 Masses heard; 520 Holy Communions; 19,024

Prayers; 6,446 Ejaculations; 391 Rosaries; and 988 Visits to the Blessed Sacrament."

But as much as Josephine loved teaching and her teachers, not to mention the children, she appreciated a break in her routine. Helping to keep the full bent bow from breaking was the summer holiday. For some twenty years, she vacationed at Goderich, Ontario, on the shores of Lake Huron. After daily Mass and Communion as usual, she relaxed by hiking through the woods, in fishing or in boating. In any memoir of her she would have wanted remembered her hosts at Goderich, the MacIntoshes, John and his wife Nora. For a more than paying-guest attachment between them and her blossomed through the years. How much the place and the people meant to her is evident from her words spoken in the hospital shortly before her death: "I wish I were in Goderich!"

Charlotte Casgrain's rambling bungalow in the White Mountains also afforded her several delightful summers. She would drive with Elizabeth to Manhattanville to visit their nun-sister Sara and then continue on to the Casgrains.

Josephine's relaxations were another key to her character. She was not the spectator type. She like to do or at least to participate. Besides hiking, fishing and boating, she played handball in her younger years, she learned to play the guitar and shared in the entertainment phase of her work, she joined in the singing which was part of her instruction schedule, and she learned how to draw and to paint, employing the talent to illustrate several of her own books. She went to an occasional moving picture and she enjoyed reading western stories.

But most of all, she loved human companionship and very frequently had friends at her home. The family memory recalls eligible young men among them. But evidently even then she had chosen otherwise. However, that no man took Josephine to the altar was not a lack in her life, and should not be viewed negatively. For Christian virginity, consecrated to increasing the kingdom of Christ, as was hers, is not primarily or essentially a negation of marital union with another human being, but the positive contracting of a marriage alliance with God.[42] In fact, it is the traditional teaching of the Church, defined by the Council of Trent, that such a state of virginity is superior to the married state.[43] Virginity as exemplified in the life and labors of Josephine Brownson represented a union with God which neither sought or needed to reproduce its kind in creatures. It had its own proper fecundity, the spiritual generation of children innumerable through her prayers, her example, her charity and her sacrifice, begetting the Son of God in countless souls. That was her life work. And that was the marriage of Josephine.

[42] John A. Hardon, S.J. *Theological Studies.* 14:622, Dec. 1953.
[43] Denziger-Bannwart. *Enchiridion Symbolorum.* #980. St. Louis. 1932.

CHAPTER NINE

"Why the golden powder
Decorates the bee."

WHEN BISHOP MICHAEL JAMES GALLAGHER WAS TRANS-
ferred from Grand Rapids to the diocese of Detroit in 1918
he was plunged into the middle of a problem. In fact, a
dilemma. As we have observed, the popularizing of the automobile resulted in the mushroom growth of the Motor City.
It also resulted in an urgent and enormous need for more
schools, more rectories, more convents, and a seminary. To
build them required millions and millions of dollars. Hence
the Bishop's dilemma. Should he conserve the credit of his
diocese, building only within its budget, and thereby risk
losing thousands of souls? Or should he borrow to the limit,
raising every cent the credit of his diocese could command,
and thus provide church and school facilities for every Catholic he could? It was a dilemma for Bishop Gallagher, but
not to him. He knew what he would do and without hesita-
tion he did it.

But while that courageous course helped the situation
immensely, it could not possibly completely resolve it. And
so there were still nearly fifty thousand Catholic children
in his diocese that could not be crowded into its Catholic
schools. They were his but he could not take care of them.
Because Josephine and her Catholic Instruction League re-

moved so much of that weight from his mind and so much of that grief from his heart, he had great affection for her. And so, gratefully for her in 1933 he besought from His Holiness Pope Pius XI the medal *Pro Ecclesia et Pontifice*. At the formal dinner given by the teachers of the C.I.L., the Bishop gave the principal address and Right Rev. Monsignor William Murphy (late Bishop of Saginaw) acted as toastmaster.

Josephine expressed her own reactions to the presentation in a letter which we quote in part: "I believe it strengthens the work to have the medal publicized as it was, and our banquet was a great success. The dinner was excellent. The room was filled with about three hundred, including nearly fifty priests. The air was vibrant with enthusiasm. The Bishop was very handsome and spoke as never before. Beautifully and strongly. The first time he has ever appeared publicly for the C.I.L. I wish he had been quoted *in toto*. He cut the ground completely from under the feet of all those who raise any kind of objection to our work." [44]

The Bishop never deviated in his support, and during the succeeding depression years, when pressure for payments on the diocesan loans was strongest and hardest to meet, he had the consolation of knowing that her work was taking care of one of his principal obligations without adding anything to his financial burden.

At the C.I.L. dinner following his death on January 20, 1937, Josephine with deep emotion declared that "Not one in this hall tonight but feels the absence of that central figure who unfailingly attended our annual dinner because by doing so he could best prove his deep interest in our work and his strong support of our efforts."

Pro Ecclesia et Pontifice: For the Church and the Holy Father. Her Bishop had given her work diocesan endorse-

[44] Letter to Rev. A. J. Heeg, S.J., Feb. 11, 1933.

ment; the Vicar of Christ now gave it the endorsement of the Church Universal. It is officially acknowledged as sharing in the teaching mission of the Church. In view of the nature of her work, no greater honor could be given her this side of heaven.

In the same year, she was accorded another public tribute. Public in presentation, but oh so affectionately personal. From the days of the fragile and uncertain beginnings of what only years later developed into the Catholic Instruction League, Josephine had been blest with the wise and prudent counsel, the financial and moral support of the Jesuits of Detroit. And, reassigned as they regularly were to various posts in various places, their thrice-welcome letters followed her right up to the very end. And so it was the tender and touching tribute of old friends, this conferring upon her of the honorary doctorate of laws by the Jesuits' University of Detroit. The presentation was made by the Very Rev. Albert H. Poetker, S.J., president of the University. Since two others [45] were likewise honored at this graduation exercises of some four hundred and fifty students, the citation and the ceremony were necessarily brief. The occasion was the fiftieth annual commencement of the University.

Further recognition of the great and lasting worth of her labors came in a telegram from the Rev. John F. O'Hara, C.S.C.,[46] president of the University of Notre Dame, announcing that she had been chosen Laetare Medalist for 1939.

It is a tradition that the recipient selects the reception date and place. Josephine chose Notre Dame as the place

[45] They were Frank Cody, superintendent of schools of the City of Detroit, and Dr. William J. Seymour, chief of staff of Eloise Hospital.
[46] Father O'Hara was consecrated Titular Bishop of Mylasa in 1940; named Bishop of Buffalo, 1945; and promoted to the See of Philadelphia, 1951.

and the date, June fourth, the Feast of the Most Holy Trinity. The secretary of the C.I.L., Miss Matilda Deane, drove her to the University.

Following Father Hugh O'Donnell's introduction, Bishop John Francis Noll, of Fort Wayne, presided over the program. He spoke in praise of the Brownsons, "a family that had distinguished itself through three generations by the defense of God's religion." The Bishop said that he had been chosen to bestow the University's "highest testimonial of recognition because he had been in a position to follow her apostolate and had even collaborated with her in the publication and dissemination of her writings." He concluded: "Receive this symbol of Catholic America's appreciation and the multitude of prayers which go with it for an abundant harvest so certain to mature from the seed that you have already sown and will continue to sow."

Father O'Hara's presentation address concluded with these words: "The University is especially happy to add your name, Miss Brownson, to the list of distinguished Catholic laymen and laywomen. Daughter of Henry F. Brownson, himself Laetare Medalist of 1892, and granddaughter of Orestes A. Brownson, eminent philosopher and publicist, whose tomb in Sacred Heart Church is one of the University's proudest treasures, you richly deserve this honor. Thirty-three years ago, with extraordinary vision and deep practical sense of the interests of the Church, you established a Catholic Instruction League in the City of Detroit. Your disinterested and unflagging devotion has carried this great work forward until you are now leading an organization of some four hundred teachers and fourteen thousand students. This splendid achievement marks you as an eminent leader in the true spirit of Catholic Action for which you have already been honored by the Papal decoration *Pro Ecclesia et*

Pontifice (given, I say, without ceremony, but none the less of enormous significance to those who know what it means). In this noblest of the works of mercy you have earned the gratitude of Catholics everywhere as well as the manifest blessing of God. On this appropriate day, the octave of Pentecost, and the feast of the Most Holy Trinity, the University begs continued blessing upon your work and proudly and joyously presents to you the Laetare Medal for this our present year of grace, 1939." [47]

A friend of the family, Mrs. Alexis Coquillard, recalls the occasion: "The Commencement Exercises had been held the previous day, and the campus seemed hushed and still. The presentation was made in Washington Hall, an old building, rich in memories. I recall thinking that Josephine's brother Philip must have come there many times as a student. The Hall was brilliantly lighted as we entered. There was a prelude of music. [48] A drop curtain of rich crimson velvet had been let down back stage and a half dozen handsomely carved chairs were grouped in a semi-circle on the stage. Miss Brownson responded to the addresses delightfully. Her remarks were gay and witty. In describing the work of the Catholic Instruction League, she laughingly mentioned how flattered Detroit felt when Boston not only let it be known that they knew of the work of the League but actually asked advice as to how they might commence such a work themselves. She spoke of her own individual part in the work as though there had been great joy in it. Yet one sensed the labor as well as the love that lay hid in that labor of love. At the conclusion of her response, she was pre-

[47] Father O'Hara's press release included this especially significant statement: "Miss Brownson was one of the first Catholics in any country to organize on an extensive scale the catechetical instruction ordered by Pope Pius X in his encyclical *Acerbo Nimis,* promulgated in 1905."

[48] Music was by the Symphony Orchestra of South Bend.

sented with a large bouquet of shell-pink roses. Then an informal reception in her honor was held in the University parlor. Several Detroiters were there: I recall seeing John Bell Moran and Henrietta O'Brien."

The award of the Laetare Medal was, of course, widely publicized and so brought her work to the attention of much of the nation. Officially the country noted and recorded the event through the interest of the Honorable Louis Charles Rabaut. He addressed the House of the Congress on March 31, 1939, in these words:

"Mr. Speaker:

I wish to have preserved in the *Congressional Record* an event of memorable significance. On Sunday, March 19, 1939, Miss Josephine Brownson, a respected and beloved citizen of my congressional district in Detroit, Michigan, was awarded the Laetare Medal by the University of Notre Dame. This honor, the highest a Catholic layman can receive in the United States, is annually bestowed by the University. . . . Both in Catholic Action and in the field of writing, Miss Brownson carries on the literary tradition of her family, begun by Orestes A. Brownson, the "Father of American Philosophy" . . . Miss Brownson's father, Henry F. Brownson, a philosopher and author, was awarded the Medal in 1892. This is the first time that a descendant of a former Medalist has received the honor. . . ." Congressman Rabaut concluded by recording "the complete honor roll of the men and women who in their particular fields of endeavor, have achieved such distinction as reflects glory upon their Catholic Faith . . . from 1883, when the Very Rev. Edward Sorin, C.S.C., founder of the University, bestowed the first Medal on the late John Gilmary Shea, eminent Catholic historian."

Most of the surviving members of that distinguished roll call were among the first to send their congratulations to the new Medalist: Mary Virginia Merrick (1915), of Washington, D. C., founder of the Christ Child Society; James Joseph Walsh (1916), of New York, physician, author, lecturer; Joseph Scott (1918), of Los Angeles, lawyer; Alfred E. Smith (1929), of New York, statesman; Frederick Philip Kenkel (1930), of St. Louis, social science; and Jeremiah D. M. Ford (1937), of Harvard, classical scholar.

Indicative of the breadth of interest in her work was the avalanche of felicitations sent her. At least a few must be mentioned here: Bishop John F. Noll, of Fort Wayne; Bishop Francis C. Kelley, of Oklahoma City; Bishop Aloisius J. Muench, of Fargo; Bishop William J. Hafey, of Scranton; Bishop James A. Griffin, of Springfield, Illinois; Bishop James E. Kearney, of Rochester; Archbishop Joseph F. Rummel, of New Orleans; Bishop Vincent Wehrle, O.S.B., of Bismarck; Bishop William L. Adrian, of Nashville; retired Bishop Mathias C. Lenihan, of Great Falls; Bishop Stephen J. Donahue, Administrator of the See of New York; Bishop Emmet J. Walsh, of Charleston; Rev. Leo De Barry, director of the Society for the Propagation of the Faith, Detroit; Rev. John J. Sigstein, founder of Our Lady of Victory Missionary Sisters; Mother Grace C. Dammann, R.S.C.J., president of Manhattanville College of the Sacred Heart, New York; Rev. James J. Daly, S.J., poet and author, University of Detroit; Rev. Francis X. Fitz Gibbon, secretary of the Confraternity of Christian Doctrine, diocese of Brooklyn; Rev. Joseph C. Flynn, S.J., spiritual director of the Jesuit Retreat League, Cincinnati; Rev. Emmet A. Hannick, pastor of St. Rose Church, Detroit; [49] Mr. John J. Murphy, of Cleveland, a

[49] Rev. Dr. Hannick had been appointed a curate to Josephine's uncle, Msgr. Van Dyke, at St. Aloysius Church, Detroit. The Monsignor had asked him to co-operate with her and thus he became familiar with her work about 1919, and he remained a loyal and generous promoter of it through the years.

trustee of the University of Notre Dame; Congressman Louis C. Rabaut; Mr. Theodore F. MacManus, publicity and author, Detroit; Miss Mary C. Mellyn, assistant superintendent of the Public Schools of Boston; Judge Thomas M. Cotter and Judge Joseph A. Moynihan, of Detroit; and many, many more. Congratulatory resolutions were sent, too, by innumerable organizations: the Catholic Evidence Guild, the League of Catholic Women (both Detroit and Grand Rapids), the Brownson Guild, Detroit, and the Brownson Circle, Chicago (both named for her grandfather), the St. Mary Alumnae of Monroe (Detroit chapter), the Franciscan Sisters of the Atonement, Greymoor, New York, the Felician Sisters of Detroit, the several communities of her old teachers: the Religious of the Sacred Heart; and, again, many, many more.

Josephine was grateful for all these gracious remembrances. But her heart was particularly touched by the labored notes in longhand from many of the little people whom she had befriended through the years.

Such as the one from "your ex-pupil and good friend," Julio E. Lanausse, who says how happy he was to see her honored and who thanks her again for the rosary and prayerbook she sent him when he was in the Signal Corps of the Canadian Armed Forces.

Or the one from Mrs. Charles E. Dwyer, of Hamilton, Ontario, written on April 7, 1939: "I remember it was about 1914. I was twelve and you were instrumental in getting me to receive Holy Communion every Sunday. Children were not encouraged at that time to go to Communion as frequently as they are now. You gave me a little button and I wore it for many years. I am proud to say that during the years I haven't forgotten your good advice." Written after twenty-five years!

But few of these can be quoted. Their warm heart's blood should not be mixed with printer's ink.

At home, the Grosse Pointe Alumnae of the Sacred Heart paid her their fellow-member's tribute. It was delivered by Clare W. Morrison, by appointment of the president Mrs. Frances Moran French.

Also at home, another. One which marked the pinnacle of her career, and its turning point.

On June 6, 1939, in the Detroit-Leland Hotel, the teachers of her own Catholic Instruction League gave her a testimonial dinner. By the presence of the Archbishop and the president of the Notre Dame Club both the Supreme Pontiff and the University were represented. To show her appreciation, she wore the medal bestowed on her by the Holy Father and the one given her by Notre Dame. Warmth was infused into the radiance of the occasion by the presence of her beloved teachers. They were more than her fellow-workers, they were a part of her, they were her other self. Side by side they had shared the divine adventure. From the precarious beginnings in the Palms' stable, through the store-quarters of the Weinman Club, on through school basements and hallway classrooms, up to the present peak of forty beautiful, modern public school buildings for their use, she and they had climbed a ladder whose rungs read prayer, and labor, and self-sacrifice. But progress in accommodations was only a progress in means to an end. And it was the end that was being climaxed and crowned here tonight. How many thousands of children, who otherwise might not have been, had they taught the knowledge and the love of God, how many marriages had they sanctified, how many prodigals had they returned to the Home of the Father, how many— but why try to read the secrets of the Book of Life! Sufficient to know that one's labors had been performed for God. But surely gratifying, too, that they have been acclaimed by those on earth best equipped to judge them. More than that, it was pure joy. And so Josephine was radiantly happy on this night.

Soon the toastmaster called upon her for a few words. She concluded, as she had begun, with a reference to the Archbishop, expressing her gratitude to him who by his presence showed his interest in her work.

He too was, of course, called upon to speak. In his reply he said he was not only interested but grateful to her for helping him in *his* work.

CHAPTER TEN

"After the first death, there is no other"

BISHOP GALLAGHER WENT TO HIS REWARD IN 1937 AND
was succeeded by Archbishop Mooney. Naturally Josephine
was concerned with the question of his attitude toward the
Catholic Instruction League.

Her work had enjoyed the personal affection of Bishop
Gallagher. He had welcomed every opportunity to praise
and encourage her in public and in the press; he had attended and spoken at all their annual dinners; he had appointed an Auxiliary to aid their work financially; and he had
besought the Holy Father for the Papal endorsement given
her by the medal *Pro Ecclesia et Pontifice*.

In verses more heartfelt than poetical a C.I.L. teacher
had emphasized this mutual esteem:

> *"O friends most dear, and did you hear*
> *The news that's going around.*
> *The C.I.L. is springing up*
> *Like mushrooms from the ground.*
>
> *"For we've a Bishop whom we love,*
> *A Bishop without fear,*
> *And he has said the children all*
> *God's holy word must hear.*

97

"I met with Bishop Gallagher
And he took me by the hand,
And he said how is the C.I.L.
And how does she stand?

"She's the best in all the country,
I'll tell the reason why:
Our Bishop is right with us
And we for him would die."

But how could it be otherwise than that Archbishop Mooney's regard for the Catholic Instruction League would be just as deep and just as sincere as his predecessor's? How could it be otherwise, for both were priests and prelates dedicated to the salvation of souls? Could either be other than grateful that Josephine had labored so long, so zealously and so effectively to inspire and direct an organization devoted to the religious instruction of thousands upon thousands of the least cared for of the Church's children in their own diocese?

There was never any question in the mind of either prelate as to the worth of Josephine's work. They just saw that work from different viewpoints: Bishop Gallagher saw it with his heart; Archbishop Mooney with his head. Bishop Gallagher had shared in the trials and tribulations of its development. When Archbishop Mooney came to Detroit the Catholic Instruction League had long been established as a nationally recognized organization. An organization whose work, however, belonged by divine right to the Church, and by the law of that Church belonged under the direction and supervision of a diocesan department, namely, the Confraternity of Christian Doctrine. And he left no doubt in the mind of anyone concerned that he was going to put it there. His words to Josephine at the C.I.L. teachers' testimonial dinner were crystal clear: He thanked her for helping him in *his* work.

Why did he move so quickly? But first, let us see why he moved at all.

We have said that the work of the Catholic Instruction League belonged by divine right to the Church. Her mission is to teach. All religious instruction is hers. It is; it has to be; and, to mean anything at all, it has to be hers inclusively and exclusively. *All* religious instruction whether it be given in church, in the school, in the rectory or convent, or even in the home by parents to their own children,—all has to be instruction in doctrine approved by the Church. Otherwise there would have been no reason at all for Christ to have founded His Church.

And, at least since the days of Pope St. Pius X, it has been the desire of the Holy See that the public exercise of this apostolate be under the supervision and direction of the Confraternity of Christian Doctrine in every diocese. In fact, that is the principal reason for the existence of that department.

In the United States the Papal directive was carried out in this manner: in 1934 our American Bishops appointed a committee, called the Episcopal Committee of the Confraternity of Christian Doctrine, at the same time organizing a National Center of the Confraternity of Christian Doctrine in Washington, D. C., as one of the departments of the National Catholic Welfare Conference. It was the business of this Committee to unify under the Confraternity of Christian Doctrine all catechetical instruction in the United States. This was a practical way of bringing about the fulfillment of

Canon 711 of the Code of Canon Law that requires the Confraternity of Christian Doctrine and it's work to be a part of every parish.

In 1935, the Bishops of the United States received an instruction from the Sacred Congregation in Rome, directing them to report the progress of the organization and work of the Confraternity of Christian Doctrine each in his own diocese, and to continue to file such reports every five years.

At the time that the Episcopal Committee of the Confraternity was established, the Bishops asked that all existing agencies for the teaching of Christian doctrine be placed under *one head,* and be known by *one name,* and be supervised by a Priest-director appointed in every diocese in the United States.

And so it is obvious that logically and fittingly that the work of Josephine's Catholic Instruction League, if the Archbishop deemed it worthy, should be part of the Confraternity of Christian Doctrine of the Archdiocese of Detroit.

But why did he step in so quickly? It really was not as quickly as it appears; the fact is, it was two years after he had come into the diocese.[50] And he had more pressing problems (such as the enormous diocesan debt) to take care of first. Sufficient to say, he got to the Catholic Instruction League as quickly as he could. Why?

Because he did not want the C.I.L. organization and personnel to be lost to his diocese, and he knew that it would be if he delayed too long.

Josephine was nearing sixty and she was suffering from a heart ailment. If she died, the C.I.L. died. For, of course, she was the C.I.L. True, in correspondence with some of her

---

[50] In contrast, the Archbishops of Chicago and Milwaukee, for example, directed the discontinuance of the name Catholic Instruction League in their diocese immediately, whereas in Detroit the name was not completely dropped until 1953, some ten years later.

friends she had protested that she was "not indispensable." But the wish was father to the thought; everyone else knew otherwise. If the Archbishop had thought less of the C.I.L. he could have simply let it die with her. But it was to prevent such a loss that he began preparing for its incorporation into his diocesan Confraternity. By doing this in time, it required only an organizational adjustment to insure the continuance of her work.

How did Josephine take it?

The first powerful impact that burst upon her brain before she could begin to rationalize dazed her. As a drowning man in the moment of his dying is said to see the highlights of his life flash across his mind's eye, so there blazed through her mind milestones on the long hard road of bringing the C.I.L. from its precarious infancy to its stalwart maturity. And now in an instant the labor of a lifetime was required to become a helpless lamb to be sacrificed on the altar of authority.

But emotional impact was quickly cushioned by character. And her letters reveal that once her mind took command, the doctrine she taught was the doctrine she practiced.

To facilitate the absorption of the Catholic Instruction League into the Confraternity of Christian Doctrine, she at once offered to resign; but the Archbishop asked her not to. She then offered to have the name Catholic Instruction League dropped; but, again, he asked her not to. He advised her to carry on as an official affiliate of the diocesan Confraternity. He knew that time would take care of those and other details.

In view of the fact that Josephine had spent not only her life but her life's earnings on her work, he saw to it that she was sent a monthly check. Typically, she consulted her spiritual adviser about it, saying that she did not know how she could keep it since she was now so often ill and unable to take an active part in the work. More and more often it began to meet the expenses of sickness.

On July 25, 1940, she wrote Father Heeg from White-field, New Hampshire, "I went as long as I could and finally collapsed, falling in a dead faint at the altar-rail during Mass."

It was, of course, her heart again. Affectionately re-turned home in easy stages by her sister Elizabeth, she re-covered sufficiently to leave late in November by train for Clearwater, Florida. She was sent for a complete rest and to avoid the risks of colds which would put an additional strain on her heart. Her devoted host in Clearwater was her cousin and life-long friend, Mary Barnard.

But rest was late in coming and care was not able to lift the weight of the overburdened years. She showed but slight improvement. Enough to read a little and to write notes home, just enough to sit out on the beach occasionally.

Her correspondence indicates that she was unaware that back home the name Catholic Instruction League was no more and her texts and method superseded. But that would have been of less moment to her than the cross she did have to bear. On her physician's orders, she remained in bed until around ten in the morning. She then asked to be taken to church. But she could not receive Holy Commun-ion, for if she was able to get to church then, she was able to get there earlier when Communion was distributed during Mass. If we do not appreciate the depth of sadness the priva-tion of this daily life-long spiritual consolation and support brought into her dying days, then little of her life has been revealed in these pages.

Nor even with the passing months did her bodily strength return. She became listless of life around her. Her worn and wasted frame languished in an alien clime. But where was her heart? "It is my dream to establish a model school where instructors may come and sit in on model classes in religion . . . There is real need for this model school."

But she knew in her heart, weak as it was, that she was beyond cure, and she longed to return home. She left in June of 1942, coming by way of New York for a last visit with her nun-sister Sally. She was scarcely settled at home when she suffered a stroke and was rushed to Jennings' Hospital. After being annointed, she rallied sufficiently to be transferred to the Convalescent Home (now Hospital) of the Sisters of Bon Secours in Grosse Pointe. Among her visitors there was Archbishop Mooney.

Josephine returned home late in September. But she was ready and willing to die. All that she could do, she had done. Death came for her before dawn on the tenth of November, 1942, at Bon Secours.

Years before, in conversation with Gertrude Healy, an intimate friend of the family as well as one of her C.I.L. teachers, Josephine had remarked that her (Josephine's) mother had been buried in the habit of the Third Order of Saint Francis. Something in the way she said it moved Miss Healy to reply that she would see to it that Josephine would be too. And now, when Josephine was being laid out for burial, Gertrude was present and suggested that she be clothed in the habit. Thus, like her mother, she came to be buried as a Franciscan Tertiary.

Immediately upon being notified of her death, Archbishop Mooney had a telegram sent to her sister Elizabeth: "Please accept sincere condolences and assurance of prayers. Deeply regret that the Bishops' meeting prevents me from being present to render tribute of appreciation of Josephine's great work for the Church through the Catholic Instruction League."

Funeral services were held on Thursday morning, November twelfth, in SS. Peter and Paul Church. The priests of this parish had encouraged and aided her first religious instruction classes in the basement of their school nearly forty years before.

Father Arthur D. Spillard, S.J., the pastor, was celebrant of The requiem High Mass. The sermon was delivered by Father John C. Ryan, archdiocesan director of the Confraternity of Christian Doctrine.

Burial was in the old Mount Elliott Cemetery, across from the Capuchin Monastery.

One wishing to visit her grave would go to the caretaker. He would show you the plot. You would take his word for it. You would have to. No headstone, no marker. Just a space of green in summer, of white in winter. Her memory as purely spiritual as her death.

For the building of the Kingdom of God upon the earth is incompatible with the honors and glories of the earth. Josephine must be bereft of adulation and organization, of power and prestige. The material must fail for the spiritual to conquer. For ultimate victory is possible in the spiritual order alone: only death can permit access to it. And "after the first death, there is no other."

Epilogue, 1955

I have finished, Josephine. All the facts that I could find are here, and all the figures. Some will wonder, Was it worth the wear? Will question, Does it matter now? For your army is disbanded and your banner bears another name. Your writings are ignored and other methods rule. Was it worth your life, Josephine?

Ah yes, infinitely yes! For work like mine can never die. It lives on in countless souls and passes its spirit into other outward forms that succeed it, merging, so to speak, in the total teaching mission of the Church. The greatest of theologians—St. Thomas Aquinas, whom I revered and whom I followed—the Angelic Doctor himself could not have asked for more.

1—Pierre Jean Desnoyers (1772–1846) Josephine's Great Grandfather

2—Orestes   Augustus   Brownson   (1803–1876)
Grandfather

3 & 4—Mrs. James A. Van Dyke (Elizabeth Desnoyers) (1815–1895)

GRANDPARENTS

5—Mr. James A. Van Dyke

6 & 7—Mrs. Henry F. Brownson and Major Henry F. Brownson
(1835–1913)

PARENTS AT MARRIAGE, 1868

8—Mrs. Henry F. Brownson

PARENTS, IN LATER LIFE, 1910

9—Henry F. Brownson, At-
torney

10—Josephine at twelve, 1892

11—Josephine at seventeen, 1897

12—Josephine at thirty-five, 1915

13—Josephine at fifty-eight, 1938

Acknowledgments

To Archbishop O'Hara for his stirring and informative Foreword.

To Father F. H. Drinkwater, editor of *The Sower,* a journal of Catholic education, and author of many teachers' aid-books, sermon notes, religious plays, etc., for his professional appraisal of Josephine's contribution to religious instruction, given in Chapter Five of this work.

To Right Rev. Msgr. Edward J. Hickey, P.A., founder of the Gabriel Richard Press, for his guidance and encouragement.

To Father George W. Paré, historian of the Archdiocese of Detroit, whose reading of the manuscript resulted in sound and subtle advice on many points.

To Father Victor F. Suren, director of the Central Bureau of the Catholic Central Verein of America, for his kind permission to include Josephine's *Stopping the Leak* as an Appendix to this book.

To Miss Matilda Deane, Josephine's Secretary for twelve years, for patiently checking over the manuscript with the author.

To the Very Rev. Charles Kelly, C.S.B., pastor of Saint Anne's, who graciously permitted use of the Registers of the parish.

To the Religious of the Sacred Heart, in particular, Rev. Mother Wansboro, of their Detroit Academy, and to Rev. Mother Healy, Mother Hemmert and Mother Ernestine Smith, of their Grosse Pointe Academy.

To Father Francis X. Canfield, librarian at Sacred Heart Seminary, and Sister M. Claudia, I.H.M., librarian at Marygrove College, both in Detroit.

To the reference staff of the Detroit Public Library.

To my wife Madeleine who, as an alumna of the Academy of the Sacred Heart in Grosse Pointe and later as a member of the staff of the Detroit Public Library, brought both of these advantages to bear on the writing of this book.

Appendix I

Stopping the Leak by Josephine Brownson

FOREWORD

HUNDREDS OF THOUSANDS OF OUR CATHOLIC CHILDREN are being lost to the Church through inadequate religious instruction. Such is the case throughout the length and breadth of our country, in the large city, in the small town, on the isolated farm. The valiant parish school cannot as yet accommodate or reach all.

Some have never had an opportunity to attend a class of religious instruction; others have attended such a class, but found the lessons so dull that the day they were confirmed, they practically bade farewell to the Church.

It is our privilege to gather these children in school or church or private home and there give them love as well as knowledge of the beauty of religion. It is within our power to exert upon them an influence that will affect their whole future life. We can stop the appalling leakage!

To teach such is not only our privilege but our duty. 'To the Greeks and to the barbarians, to the wise and the unwise, I am a debtor.'

If the mill will never grind with the water that has passed, neither can we ever bring back the children we are letting slip through our fingers now.

Nihil Obstat: F. G. Holweck, Censor.
St. Louis, December 14, 1925
Imprimatur: ✠ Johannes J. Glennon, Archieppus Sti. Ludovici.
Die 16a. Decembris, 1925

In a few years priests will be devoting their lives and exerting every ounce of their strength to bring into the Church by missions and convert classes a few of the many that are ours now for the asking.

Oh, let us shake off this torpor and stretch out a hand to save the souls of thousands of little children that are hourly perishing at our door. You do not see them? Have you ever looked? Walk along any street and question any group of children you meet. You will find among them children who have been robbed of their birthright, children who have been told nothing of the inheritance that is theirs, children who at a word from us will attend a Catholic school, children who will gladly come to our instructions, children whose parents we can bring back to the household of the Faith, children whose young lives Death will claim and who will die without having received a Sacrament.

"But," you may say, "this is work for nuns and priests and not for us layfolk." No, in the present critical situation our standing-army of priests and nuns is not sufficient and the call is out for volunteers.

Can we stand idly by and watch a little child drown because its parents are the ones responsible for it?

The following thoughts are offered as suggestions to good teaching. If you have never taught, learn from them how to teach and help stop the leak.

TEACHING RELIGION

A schedule is essential. It introduces system and with system comes order and with order interest. No teacher can fail who is prepared every week to carry out the schedule. Right here lies the secret of teaching religion successfully— one must be prepared. The majority of teachers are not prepared. They do not think over the schedule and rehearse what they will do and say when in presence of their class.

Some will spend the whole hour drilling on prayers. This kills a class and the attendance dwindles. Others wait to receive inspiration whilst hearing the lesson. Still others devote the entire time to asking over and over the dry questions of the catechism.

When a teacher is unprepared and does not know how she will spend the hour, the class becomes unattentive and unruly. When a teacher is prepared, she has confidence in herself and this confidence reacts upon the children, and whilst she passes rapidly from one matter to the other, she carries the class with her and will receive great attention.

To teach religion well, no amount of preparation is too great, no sacrifice too costly. It is a stupendous work, for its effects are as far-reaching as the limits of eternity. Is not this worth the very best that is in us? Is it not worth foregoing some pygmie pleasure—a card or theatre party, a tea, a lecture—or to fight a headache or a cold that we may never be found missing at our post when the hour sounds for us to train citizens for the Heavenly Jerusalem?

Let us not be frightened by the amount of preparation required of us. Love knows no labor. Let us be convinced of one truth: we shall get out of our class all we put into it and only what we put into it. If we drop into our class weekly, without preparation, we shall accomplish very little.

You may ask: "What is this preparation?" It consists in thinking, planning, on an average of two hours for every hour of class. You may say: "This is a great deal." I answer: "This is a great work." You may object: "I haven't time." I rejoin: "Then you are just the one for the work. Only those whose lives are crowded find time to work for God."

You can prepare whilst walking in the street, riding in a street car, waiting for an appointment, and so on. Soon the things you see and hear, the books you read, will furnish material for your instructions.

Unless the class becomes a joy to pupils and to teacher, it will never be the success it should be. And it will be a joy to us only when we love our children and love to work for them. This mutual love will do more for their eternal salvation than memorizing the entire catechism.

A little personal interest in the individual members of the class will evoke a warm response. To see the readiness with which children perform heroic acts of self-denial, to see the depths of piety and devotion we have awakened, to see little cheeks wet with tears when we speak of the sufferings of Christ—all this would draw love from the heart of an oak.

The schedule should be put in operation the first time the class is held. Some teachers wait for a satisfactory attendance. This is like waiting for a bite before baiting the hook.

How often one hears a teacher say: "I started my class. Only three or four children came so I let them go home as soon as I had enrolled them. I told them to come back next week and bring others." Does the trapper who finds in his snare a single fox with glorious brush, free him and say: "Come again and bring your friends?" We must hold every child we get by interesting him at once.

We should exert ourselves to the utmost, though we spend our powers on a single pupil. One child is worth it and moreover, if we do this, our class will rapidly grow. Our classes do not remain small because the children fail to come, but because we fail to interest those who do come. If we keep every child that we enroll, our classes will be large.

TEACHER AND CLASS

The same schedule should be followed for the entire class. The time is too short to admit divisions. If obliged to have children greatly differing in age and ability and knowledge, give an instruction simple enough for the least advanced and rich enough in material to interest the most advanced. And if the catechism is being studied, keep the entire class on the same lesson. Those who already know it, need not study.

I once walked into a classroom and found the larger children sitting behind the teacher's back. She answered my question by saying that they knew more than the others. Knowledge was evidently its own reward!

Never let one of the pupils hear the lesson of the class or of part of the class. Children do not care to recite to one of their own companions and moreover we should carry on the entire class ourselves.

I have in mind a high school student. I asked him whether he were a Catholic and he answered: "I used to be." Then he told me that he had made his First Communion and attended Sunday School, but that the catechism lessons were uninteresting, that the teacher allowed him to hear the lesson. It was a case of the blind leading the blind, and both the boy and his parents have now drifted from the Church.

Never let the children study during the class-hour. They should then get what only we can give them.

The schedule should be started on time. It is criminal for a teacher to commence five, ten, fifteen minutes late when the eternal salvation of the children is at stake. Some teachers leisurely talk with one another whilst the children are waiting and will likely go home feeling that they went a long distance for very little. Others make it a point to call on priest or sisters just before class and of course remain longer than they had expected to remain.

Never allow an interruption. Let everyone know that

you can not be interviewed during the hour of class. Each class must be carried on as perfectly and made as interesting as possible.

To cause the children to love their class will do more for them than to teach them to define the indefectibility of the Church. If they love their class, they will love their religion. And they will love their class if we are thoroughly prepared. Let us take a half-hour a week to think about our children, going over their names in our attendance-book and checking up each one, seeing what means we can devise to avoid some blunder of the past, to induce a certain child to attend Sunday Mass, to prevail upon another to say his prayers, to make another more regular in attendance, and so on.

Frequently when I ask a teacher how many pupils she has, she stops to calculate with the result that she cannot say accurately. At once I know that she is not giving to her class more than one-tenth of the interest and love that she could give.

THE SCHEDULE

Taking attendance .... 5 minutes
Recitation and assignment of lesson ...... 15 minutes
Questions regarding weekly practice,
    attendance at Mass, and so on .... 5 minutes
Prayers .... 10 minutes
Instruction .... 20 minutes
Hymn .... 5 minutes

ATTENDANCE

Open each class by taking the attendance as well as the names and addresses of all newcomers. Never omit this important detail. Do not postpone it until the end of the class lest it be neglected. Sometimes the children drift in for a lesson and never come again and are lost to us because we have failed to secure their name and address. The names and addresses should be kept in a durable book where we may mark the attendance in ruled spaces for the entire year. Teachers have an inborn repugnance for an attendance-book and many either come to class without a pencil or at best keep the enrollment on various scraps of paper.

The same style of attendance-book can be used by all teachers and these books may be collected at the end of the year by the head of the center. A card catalogue may furnish name, address, etc., of every child in a given center.

It is sometimes necessary to install an entire new staff of teachers in a center and if the names and addresses of former pupils are not on file, the whole center has to be built up anew. These cards also give a necessary check on all classes and great care should be given to looking up last year's pupils who have not returned.

Of prime importance is regular attendance and punctuality on the part of the teacher herself. Irreparable harm is done a class by her absence and tardiness. One should have recourse to a substitute only in cases of absolute necessity. If possible the teacher should be the first in the class-room. Once let the children gain possession and they have scored and we have lost.

We should make friends of the Sisters in the parish where we teach and win them over to the right view of our work. Many of them feel that we are enemies of the Parish School. On the contrary, we realize that only in the Catholic school can the children receive the whole loaf of which we can give only the crumbs. Facts prove that children do not leave the parish school to come to us, but that many leave us to enter the parish school.

We must so win the favour of the Sisters that on the rare occasions when our absence is unavoidable, we may ask them to conduct our class. They can do much for us in many ways if once they realize that we interfere with no one, but, like Ruth, "go into the field and glean the ears of corn that escape the hands of the reapers, wheresoever we shall find grace with a householder that will be favorable to us."

Diverse methods may be employed to increase the attendance. Inquire about the brothers, sisters, cousins, friends, neighbors, school-mates of the children. To save time, this should be done outside the hour of class. Children are not their brothers' keepers and may say nothing of a brother or sister at home who is in need of instruction unless we question them pointedly.

One may have a rubber stamp made with a suitable device and stamp little white tickets. Each child receives one each time he is present. When he has five blue tickets, he may exchange them for one red ticket. At the end of the year, all having a red ticket may enjoy an outing or receive a prize or draw for a prize.

An extra ticket may be given for every two new pupils that a child brings.

Or, a prize may be promised to each child whose attendance has been perfect for the year since the day of entrance.

Or, a button stamped with a holy picture may be given to a child the third time he is present. When he has worn the button at five lessons, he may exchange it for an aluminum scapular medal. When he has worn the medal ten lessons, he may exchange it for a silver medal. When he has worn the silver medal at twenty-five lessons, he may exchange it for a gold medal. This may help to keep them with us for two years, as it will necessitate attendance at forty-three lessons.

Or, a rosary may be stamped on card-board and a card given to each child the second time he attends. At each succeeding lesson, he receives a glass bead to be sewn at home on the stamped bead. An extra bead may be given if he brings a new pupil to class. When the rosary is completed, it may be brought to class and he may then receive a real rosary.

Teachers should send a postal card or a message to absentees or, best of all, call at their homes.

When possible, the person in charge of a center should not teach. She should be free to receive new pupils, get the total attendance of the center at the end of the hour, and so on. When not needed in the school, she should take her stand on a street corner or in front of a candy-store and waylay passing children. In this way she can increase the attendance marvelously and discover families that have drifted from the Church.

Avoid excessive prize-giving. I know one teacher who gives a picture to every child every time he attends. What will she do when the children have become surfeited with pictures? Children place upon things whatever value we place. Give few prizes and let them be rewards for much effort. Crucifixes, rosaries, scapular-medals, holy-water fonts, prayer-books, the New Testament, the Following of Christ, artistic religious pictures framed, and Catholic books are splendid prizes and worth working a whole year to obtain. Yet the tendency is to load the children with caricatures of various saints.

A Christmas party and a June outing should be given to every class. The children should be promised the former as early as September and the latter in January, as incentives to regular attendance. These parties should be simple. Once give an elaborate party, in a burst of generosity, and you have set a standard to which you and your successors will ever after be chained.

Starting a Center

There are various ways of starting a center. It is a great help, when we have obtained the pastor's permission, to have him announce the opening of classes from the pulpit and urge all to look up children in their neighborhood. Also we may discover the names of two or three families who need us and go to their homes. Or we may go to any house in the district and acquire information regarding the neighborhood. I find that the quickest way is to approach a public school at the time of dismissal or to stand at a street corner or to walk around the block. Speak to any child regarding his grade in school, nationality or church attendance. A crowd will soon gather.

It will not suffice to merely tell the children when and where they may meet you for instructions. Take them with you at once and start them. If possible, have a teacher in readiness at the center who will interest these first comers at once whilst you go off for others.

Promote Devotion to the Sacred Heart

It will be to our advantage to establish the League of the Sacred Heart and to hold meetings every First Friday in addition to our regular weekly class. Each teacher may conduct her own class or a general mass meeting may be held with one teacher in charge.

Children are wonderful promoters among their own

families and neighbors and the establishment of the League among them will bring success to our labors.

Let the children invite their friends to these meetings and we may thus get acquainted with many who rightfully belong to us.

Have the intention-sheet hung where they can mark their good works and intentions. Receive the reports of the Promoters. Give a little talk on the League. As new members arrive, arrange to speak to them apart on the duties of the League and do not weary the older members by a constant repetition of the requirements of the Three Degrees. Encourage all who have made their First Communion to receive Holy Communion on the First Friday.

We can separate the children according to the degree to which they belong, but if we are not able to place three lively teachers in charge, it is best to keep the children together.

Then tell thrillingly the life of a martyr or of any other saint. There are so many beautiful lives, which it will really benefit the children to hear, that we ought never, even at our parties, waste time telling about the prince that turned into a frog or the pig that could not find his way home, etc. It will cost us some little labor to familiarize ourselves with the lives of the martyrs and other saints that will be most interesting and appropriate for children, but we shall be well repaid. It would be well to store our minds with nine or ten such lives so as to be prepared for emergencies. Or, read an interesting chapter from some good book so that the children will be stimulated to read the rest for themselves. For example, read one of Father Finn's or Father Spaulding's books or *Blind Agnes* or a chapter from *Fabiola* or *Callista* and tell those interested to ask for the book at the Public Library; or tell some story about a child that will stimulate imitation.

If, whilst you tell the story or read the book, you let the children eat a sugar-bun or suck a stick of candy, the meeting will be a success.

Arrange to have two or three of the more talented entertain the others at these First Friday gatherings; as, by playing the piano or the violin or singing some religious song or speaking some religious poem.

Lend to those who can sing, some of our beautiful hymns to take home and learn. Find out those who like to recite and give them some worth-while poem to memorize.

Mothers love to have their children afford entertainment when they go calling, and it is pitiful to hear their repertoire.

We can do real good by sending our children out to homes we can never reach, with little voices tuned to the Catholic Faith.

Make the meeting gay and happy, so that the First Friday of the month will be a red-letter day for them through life.

RECITATION

It is well for the ordinary class of American-born children to study the catechism. Never break ground with a catechism, but assign only such lessons as treat subjects they have already heard in the instructions. In this way, their first and lasting impressions will be rich and attractive, which they will not be if they form their own from the dry words of the text. Thus it may take ten weeks for children to learn their prayers. In the meantime the teacher has given ten instructions, so that when the first chapter is reached, it is nothing more than a summary of knowledge already acquired and the class will read many things between the lines.

Again, for example, do not explain the meaning of the Hail Mary until the instruction on the Annunciation has been given; nor assign a lesson on the Commandments until the instruction on Moses' receiving the Commandments has been given.

If the class is composed of foreigners or of children who have difficulty in memorizing, it may be wiser to omit the catechism. It will be enough for them to learn in class the few essentials by dint of repetition. After all, why waste valuable time in any class, forcing children to memorize to-day what they will forget tomorrow? Is it not sufficient for any child who has not the advantage of daily drills in a Catholic school, to have thoroughly memorized, when he leaves us, the Prayers, the Commandments of God and of the Church, the names and definitions of the Sacraments and the definition of the Mysteries of the Trinity and Incarnation?

But, whenever a lesson is assigned, it should be short. For example: One-half of the Our Father, or the Hail Mary or three or four questions in the Catechism.

Once a month, the subject of one of the preceding instructions may be used as the subject of a composition for the children who are able to write. Let them write the compositions at home. The teacher might read the best written essay to the class and award a prize.

To save time, it may be advisable, in some cases, to change the order of the schedule and let each child recite his lesson as he arrives. When all have entered, the recitation will be practically over. Children are not interested in their companions' recitation. But whenever the recitation is held, the children should see us mark their success or failure in our attendance book. Or, if they have handed in a written lesson, we should hand back last week's paper corrected.

Questions Regarding Weekly Practice, Etc.

Never omit questioning the class regarding attendance at Sunday Mass, fidelity to daily prayers and frequent aspirations, after you have started them on these practices. If a child has made an effort to go to Mass or so say his prayers, and that week we omit asking, he will be disappointed and perhaps discouraged; whereas, if he is sure that he will have an opportunity to raise his hand he will be stimulated to act.

Do not ask individually but generally, so that the ones who have been remiss will not be specially noticed by the others. Do not hold up any child for the disapproval of the others. Encouragement will accomplish more than denouncement. A little word after class, spoken to a child in private, will have far more affect than a long harangue in front of the class. For example: You may have a boy whom you cannot persuade to hear Mass. Speak to him after class. Tell him where and when he can meet you and accompany you to Mass and say that you will have a little prayer-book for him, but not to tell this to the others. He is an unusual boy, if you do not win him.

One of our teachers found the following simple device effective. She urged the children to have 100% attendance at Sunday Mass. When they came for their lessons, she asked how many had been to Mass and then wrote the percentage on the board. In time she got her 100%.

Did our children come from homes where meat is never eaten on Friday and where their parents never fail to lead them by the hand to Mass on Sunday, we might show horror should they manage to offend in either of these respects. But to tell little children (or even big ones at first) whose parents eat meat on Friday and seldom or never attend Mass on Sunday, that they sin in doing likewise, is wrong and unfair to them.

Without mention of sin, let us find out home-conditions first, and little by little lead the children to coax their parents not to have meat on Friday, because fine, strong Catholics give it up to show that they love Jesus; and gradually we can get them to hear Mass by telling them that all good Catholics, like brave soldiers, face snow and rain and fight all obstacles to attend Sunday Mass.

Only when these two habits have become fixed and the children are old enough to be responsible, should we hammer in the awfulness of the mortal sin committed by offending in these respects without excuse.

On the other hand, if we tell the children who seldom or never hear Sunday Mass that they are sinning mortally, they will get the idea that mortal sin is nothing terrible and quite impossible to avoid.

Find out from the pastor what seats in church can be reserved for our children and try to secure front seats. After class take the children to church and place them as they may place themselves on Sunday and tell them exactly at what hour they should come. Then inform the ushers so they may help to assemble the children rather than help to keep them away, as sometimes happens.

We are aiming to have the children form the life-long habit of hearing Sunday Mass, receiving Holy Communion at least weekly, saying their morning and night prayers and making frequent aspirations during the day. Their fidelity through life will depend upon our fidelity to questioning them on these points. Teach them what prayers they should say in the morning and what prayers at night. Give them the minimum and let those who wish add to it. Urge fidelity to morning and night prayers, but do not tell them it is a sin every time they omit them, because it is not.

Teach them some short aspirations and start them out saying two a day, the next week three and so on until they reach ten. Then urge them to say more, but not less than ten daily, and get them into the way of offering to God their joys and disappointments and sufferings.

Teach them to make little acts of kindness, and especially during Lent and Advent, teach them to make little acts of self-denial.

Why not have in each class or in each center, a mite-box for our Catholic Missions? The Society of the Propagation of the Faith, 109 E. 38th St., New York, will gladly furnish mite-boxes free of charge. $5.00 will ensure the rescue and baptism of a Chinese baby. And the class may choose the name by which the baby will be known for all eternity. In one of our centers the boys and girls compete and the winners name the baby. Last year these children bought five babies.

Let us teach our children to spend their pennies to save the souls of their little brothers and sisters in far off lands, who else will never see the dear Christ Who died for all.

PRAYERS

Make the recitation of prayers short and snappy. Employ various devices. If it is a normal class, able to study at home, let them recite their lesson in chorus two or three times. Then let one child start the recitation. Interrupt him by calling out the name of another child who must quickly continue the recitation. Then call on a third child and so on. Go over and over the prayer in this manner and include by way of review some prayer already learned. The object is to keep the whole class alert. If the class is large and we allow each one to recite the day's prayer in turn, all but the child reciting are restless.

Or, let all stand as in a "spell-down." Name one to start a given prayer. When you say "Next" the next one must continue or sit down. Write on the board the name of the victor.

Always conclude by having the class recite in chorus—in an intelligent manner, not in sing-song fashion—all the prayers in order as far as learned.

If the class does not study at home, let them learn four or five lines of the prayers every week in class. Let them repeat after you a given part, again and again; then in chorus without you, twice, three times. Then call on some one to recite alone; then all together again; then another solo, and so on.

Or write the words on the board. Let them read the words singly and in chorus. Or ask: Who can tell me the sixth word of the Our Father? The tenth word of the Hail Mary? Who can write on the board the fifteenth word of the Creed? And so on.

Or write on the board "I believe in the Holy Ghost" and say: "Whoever can recite the part of the Creed that follows these words, may come and erase what I have written." Or let several children go to the board and write the portion of the prayers you have assigned to each. Then let others take their place at the board and correct the work.

Flash cards, or cards on which a word or a phrase of a prayer is written, may be used in many ways.

When the class has learned all the prayers, let them at each lesson recite them in chorus slowly, distinctly, and intelligently. Keep adding to this nucleus what they should remember for life, as certain aspirations, the Angelus, the Commandments of God and of the Church, the definitions of the Mystery of the Blessed Trinity and of the Incarnation, the names of the Sacraments and the definition of each. Thus, when they have learned about the Blessed Trinity, follow up each recitation of prayers by the question: What do you mean by the Blessed Trinity? When they have learned about the Incarnation, add the following questions: What do you mean by the Incarnation? Which person of the Blessed Trinity became man? How many persons is Christ? How many natures has Christ? Was the Son of God always man? Always God? Has the Holy Ghost a body? Has the Son of God a body? Did He always have a body? Hasn't the Father a body? Is the Son of God really man? How long ago did He become man? Who is His Mother? Did the Mother of God live before God lived? How then could she be His Mother? Why did God become man? Did the whole of God become man? Did the Father and the Holy Ghost become man? And so on.

This can all be rapidly done in ten minutes. The object is endless repetition without weariness.

Some let the children kneel to recite the prayers. This is often conducive to disorder, in which case it is better to have the class sit in order with folded hands.

Frequently as the time nears for a large class to make their First Communion, the teacher discards the schedule and devotes the entire period to the arduous task of hearing prayers individually. This could be avoided by starting the examination weeks earlier and keeping three or four children after each class for examination and dividing the others in small groups and assigning to them a certain day and hour for their examination.

THE INSTRUCTION

The instruction is the backbone of the whole lesson. It should be thought over and studied much as one would prepare to play a part on the stage. Posture, gestures, tone of voice, choice of expression, all make a deep impression on the child. If the teacher allows herself to be carried away by her subject, the class will be spellbound. If the teacher has fallen in love with the beauty of God and religion, the children will listen entranced.

It is far better to tell the instruction than to read it, for children are more interested in listening to what is told, and the teacher herself will thus do better work and get many inspirations as she is speaking.

Should the teacher give the instruction standing or sitting? Some prefer to sit and have the children form a circle. Others can grow enthusiastic in speaking only when standing. Each one must determine how she can obtain the best results. However, the teacher should always be in full view of each child.

When possible, a classroom should always be used, otherwise chairs can be placed in rows four or five deep. This arrangement lends a certain formality conducive to good teaching.

Father Sheehan somewhere speaks of the indelible impression made by niceties of expression. He relates an instance of an uneducated peasant, who had treasured through a lifetime a sentence he once heard in a sermon, because it was expressed in well-chosen language.

In confirmation of this, let me tell an incident. In giving an instruction to teachers on the Fall of the Angels, I used a word which I thought peculiarly fitting and expressive. Of course, I did not tell the teachers this. One day a teacher showed me a little composition written by one of her pupils and said: "I gave my class the instruction on the Angels. One little girl was so interested that the next week she presented me with an envelope. On opening it, I found that she had gone home and written the instruction. Here it is."

I read the little composition and there was the very word, third hand, which I had selected so carefully.

To this same teacher came a little new pupil one day, saying: "I have come because I heard you were so interesting."

What to do and What to Avoid

It is a great mistake to present a teacher with a catechism and tell her to teach. As well might one present a man with a compass and tell him to sail the ship.

Most teachers cling to the catechism as to a life-preserver, and bereft of it would surely sink. They hold so tenaciously to the catechism because they do not know what else to do. It frees them from the necessity of thinking, the necessity of preparing.

Again, teachers assume that if children can be made to masticate the hard shell of set words given in a catechism, they will unconsciously digest the kernel of knowledge within. They feel, as Bishop Bellord suggests, like the Chinese apothecary, who, lacking the necessary ingredients to fill a prescription, makes his patient swallow the paper.

Again, the fact that we have partaken of well-cooked viands does not mean that we can prepare them; nor does the fact that we have been well instructed mean that we can teach. But as we can acquire the former art, so can we acquire the latter, though never can we all measure up to the same standard.

I should prefer to assign one hundred children to one good teacher than ten children to each of ten poor teachers.

We must grade our children and give our teachers the course of study they are to follow. Until other courses are ready, I would suggest five courses. Grade any child entering a center according to his grade in school, regardless of whether he had made his First Communion or not. If a child enters who is in:

The 1st or 2nd Grade, place him in Course 1.
The 3rd or 4th Grade, place him in Course 2.
The 5th or 6th Grade, place him in Course 3.
The 7th or 8th Grade, place him in Course 4.
The 9th, 10th, 11th or 12th Grade, place him in Course 5.

The first four Courses prepare a child for Confession, First Communion and Confirmation according to his capacity. Yet each of these Courses has enough material not found in the others to prevent monotony. Even if a child has made his First Communion, these Courses will be new to him.

Only those who have successfully completed Course 4 may enter Course 5. A high school student who has not made his First Communion, must take Course 4.

At the end of the year, give passing slips to those only who know thoroughly the essentials of the Course they have completed. It is well to give written tests except in Course 1. Those who pass the test for Course 4 are graduated and receive a diploma and a gold pin.

COURSE 1

Use outline with 24 Brown pictures for 36¢. Memorize Our Father, Hail Mary and Act of Contrition. No catechism is used.

COURSE 2

Prayers: Memorize the Glory and the Creed.
Recitation: "Learn of Me." (A simple catechism.)
Instructions: "Feed My Lambs."

Course 3

Prayers: Memorize the Acts and the Confiteor, definition of Blessed Trinity and of Incarnation, Ten Commandments, Six Commandments of Church, name and definition of each Sacrament, Angelus, aspirations.

Recitation: Spend the time on written home-work.

Instructions: "Catholic Bible Stories." Children may be loaned copies of this book and prepare a chapter at home each week and hand in written answers to questions about the previous lesson. These written lessons should be corrected and handed back the next week.

Course 4

Prayers: Review all that memorized in Course 3. Use "To the Heart of the Child."

Course 5

Prayers: Review all that was memorized in Course 3.

Sell to each a copy of the New Testament. Discuss the Sacraments at length and in order, the pupils reading from the Gospels references to each. For recitation, have pupils memorize the verses that are the chief authority for each Sacrament. In like manner study the establishment of the Church, the Primacy of Peter. Teachers will find "The Christ, the Son of God," by Fouard, of great help in preparation of the day's lesson.

Have a large wall-map of the Holy Land and read and discuss the Acts of the Apostles.

Hymns

We need music. It attracts and elevates. We may either close the lesson with a hymn, or, if we have to wait five or ten minutes for the children to assemble, we may utilize that time by singing.

The other day I visited a center for colored children. At the end of the hour, I sang a hymn and it was remarkable how quickly they picked it up. They went out into the street singing to the Mother of God, and as I walked home between two tiny blacks, Magnolia and Dazolene, I caught from them too the same refrain. Surely such a powerful means for good should not be neglected.

SUPPLEMENTARY WORK
QUIZZING

Whilst we continue elaborating new points in our instructions we must never give up driving in essentials already studied. In addition to the questions with which we must never fail to follow up the recitation of prayers, as already observed, it is well to ask a few questions on the last instruction as a prelude to the instruction of the day.

A few minutes' quizzing may come in conveniently if we happen to finish the instruction of the day in less than the allotted time. Indeed, it may be well every seven or eight weeks, or when for some cause, as stormy weather, a large number of the class is absent, to omit the instruction and have a quiz class in its stead. Let us fire off the questions rapidly and from every angle. The whole class must be aroused and spurred into thought. Let us corner them if we can.

At first we shall be able to lead them into contradictions and absurdities because they are not thinking, but guessing answers from our tone of voice. When they discover that they can get no clue to the truth from our questions, they will begin to think and only then will they begin to understand.

I was once asked to take a class in which the pupils had made their First Communion and were from twelve to fifteen years of age. I questioned them on the Sacraments. Some knew by rote that the Sacraments had been made by Christ, but when they saw that apparently I favored the view that others besides Our Lord had made a Sacrament, they showed wonderful familiarity with the names and lives of the popes, one going so far as to assert that Leo VIII had instituted the Sacrament of Matrimony. What her attraction was for Leo VIII I do not know. Doubtless she had never heard of him. At any rate, it is quite safe to guess that at the end of that quiz they knew positively that the Sacraments had been made by Christ and by Him alone.

It is sometimes well to question rapidly regarding a number of doctrines so as to summarize the chief articles of faith. It is well again to confine one's questions to a single dogma, such as the Trinity, Incarnation, Church, or one of the Sacraments.

Thus, on the Church: Did Christ make a Church? Prove it. Did Christ make more than one Church? How do you know this? Why did Christ not make more than one Church? What is the name of Christ's Church? How do you know that the Catholic Church is the one Christ made? About how many different churches are there? Who made these other churches? Aren't these churches as good as the Catholic Church? Why not? Who only has the right to make a church? Why? Does it make any difference to which church one belongs? Why? Is it right for a non-Catholic to become a Catholic? Why? Is it right for a Catholic to give up his church? Why not? And so on.

Once in a while the quiz class may be conducted after the manner of a spell-down and a prize given to the victor.

CONCLUSION

And now, dear reader of this little outline, may I ask whether you are a member of the Catholic Instruction League? If you are, will you not interest one other in its work? If you are not, will you not join or organize the League in your locality?

O, do not refuse to add your strength to ours in stopping the leak! With your help, the leakage will be less!

Appendix II

Catholic Instruction League, President and Executive Board, 1934

Josephine Brownson, President
Mary Derum, Vice-President
Angela Roe, Second Vice-President
Mabel Burkheiser, Treasurer
Loretta Cronin
Matilda Deane
Amelia Hensien
Mary Morgan
Mrs. Harry C. O'Neill
Mrs. Edward Ouellette
Irene Ryan
Winifred Skiffington
Theresa Waters

A few of the other veteran members, some with more than a quarter century of service in the C.I.L.:

Mary Banashok, Mary Brady, Dorothy Jungwirth, Mrs. Joseph Kennedy, Mrs. Patrick Kenny, Mrs. Ralph H. Kirby, Joan McDonald, Alice Mueller, Margaret Walsh, Margaret Frawley, Gertrude Healy, Veronica Linskey, Helen Luney,

Aileen O'Connor, Mary O'Shea, Ann Schneider, Mrs. Herbert Stringer, Mary Sullivan.

The C.I.L. Auxiliary, Charter Board, 1934
Rev. William P. Schulte
Rev. Stanley S. Skrzycki, LL.D.
Rev. Leo J. Chapman
Rev. Leo De Barry, S.T.D.
Miss Josephine Brownson, LL.D.
Miss Mary Derum
Mrs. Charles T. Fisher, Jr.
Mrs. Joseph L. Hickey
Mrs. Charles L. Palms, Jr.
Mrs. Leonard L. Lesczynski
Mrs. Bartholomew A. Seymour

Appendix III

JOSEPHINE'S CATHOLIC INSTRUCTION LEAGUE WAS AB-
sorbed into the Detroit Archdiocesan Confraternity of
Christian Doctrine. Its 1954 report, released by the Right
Rev. Monsignor John C. Ryan, director:

58,781 Catholic children outside of parish school receiving religious instruction regularly from 952 nuns and
882 lay teachers.

The report also revealed that in sixteen years fourteen
parishes had been established in areas served in a number
of instances by the instruction Centers of the Confraternity.[52]

Every year on November tenth, the anniversary of
Josephine's death, Monsignor Ryan has offered a High Mass
for her in St. Aloysius Church, faithfully attended by her
relatives, teachers and friends.

[52] *The Michigan Catholic.* April 8, 1954.

BIBLIOGRAPHY

BOOKS BY JOSEPHINE BROWNSON

Learn of Me series: 8 books: 1, Come unto Me; 2, Feed my Lambs; 3, Come and See; 4, Keep my Commandments; 5, Thou art Peter; 6, Living Water; 7, I am the Vine; 8, To the Heart of the Child. Our Sunday Visitor.

Living Forever; il. by Anna P. Woollett, R.S.C.J. 1928, Macmillan.

Catholic Bible Stories from the Old and New Testaments; pref. by Bishop Francis C. Kelley. 1919, Extension Press.

Stopping the Leak. 1943, Central Bureau Press.

ARTICLES BY HER

The Grading of Religion Classes for Public School Children. Journal of Religious Instruction, 11:876–880, May 1932.

The Other Half: a series of articles in the Acolyte Sept. 3, Sept. 17, Oct. 1, Oct. 29, Nov. 26, and Dec. 10, 1932.

Teaching the Other Half. Journal of Religious Instruction, 1: 471–76, June 1931.

Little Joachim's Visit to Bethlehem, signed Josephine Van Dyke. (A Christmas short story). Ave Maria, 75:797–798, Dec. 21, 1912.

WRITINGS ON HER

Josephine Van Dyke Brownson, Alumna; by Marie Leslie Seymour. Journal of the Associated Alumnae of the Sacred Heart, 2:63–67, Oct. 1937.

Josephine Van Dyke Brownson; by Monica Weadock Porter. 32p. 1948, Manhattanville College.

Josephine Van Dyke Brownson; by Dorothy Jungwurth. Journal of Religious Instruction, 14:568–572, Feb. 1944.

Medalist Josephine Brownson; by John W. Maney, Jr. Queen's Work, 32:5, 31, June 1940.

Trumpet Call; by Rev. F. H. Drinkwater. The Sower, No. 192, pp. 72–75, July 1954.

Catholic School Journal, 39:15A, May 1939.

Catholic World, 149:237, May 1939.

America, 60:602, April 1, 1939.

Extension, 33:29, May 1939 (includes her portrait).

Current Biography, 1940. pp. 113–114. H. W. Wilson Co. (id.)

American Catholic Who's Who, 1942–1943. vol. 5, Romig.

Catholic World, 156:357, Dec. 1942 (obituary).

SOME REVIEWS OF HER BOOKS

To the Heart of the Child:

Rev. G. Pierse, Irish Theological Quarterly. Jan. 1919.

Catholic World, 109:125, April 1919.

Commonweal, 5:27, Nov. 10, 1926.

American Ecclesiastical Review, 59:642–643, Dec. 1918.

Dominicana, pp. 44–45. March 1919.

Living Forever:

Catholic World, 129:380, June 1929.

Learn of Me

Ave Maria, 43:795, June 20, 1936.

ON THE BROWNSON FAMILY

For complete references to books and articles on them, see *The Guide to Catholic Literature.* volumes from 1940– (covering 1888–).

Index

64- 240

921
B824R

Date Due			

Romig, Walter.
Josephine Van Dyke Brownson.

MOUNT MARY COLLEGE
LIBRARY
Milwaukee 10, Wisconsin